Dickens and the Dialectic of Growth

DICKENS
AND THE
DIALECTIC OF GROWTH

Badri Raina

The University of Wisconsin Press

Published 1986

The University of Wisconsin Press
114 North Murray Street
Madison, Wisconsin 53715

The University of Wisconsin Press, Ltd.
1 Gower Street
London WC1E 6HA, England

First printing

Printed in the United States of America

For LC CIP information see the colophon

ISBN 0-299-10610-1

FOR

Tulsi, my mother

Tatha Ji, my father

AND

the rest of our beautiful family

2303159

Contents

Preface   ix

Acknowledgments   xi

1   Introduction   3

2   *Oliver Twist:* The Critical Problem   21

3   *Nicholas Nickleby* and *The Old Curiosity Shop:*
The Split Self-Image   36

4   *Martin Chuzzlewit:* A Note   58

5   *Dombey and Son:* The Critical Self-Image   62

6   *David Copperfield:* The Price of Success   77

7   The Novels of the Fifties: A Connecting Note   102

8   *Great Expectations:* Being as Relatedness   108

9   *Our Mutual Friend:* A Concluding Note   130

Notes   141

Index   165

Preface

This essay on Dickens seeks to return the reader to familiar matters in the author's life and times. It hopes to recover a sense of the quality and the scope of Dickens' struggle to understand himself and, simultaneously, the history of which he was a part.

To the extent that my exegesis proceeds as the demonstration of an operative dialectic within Dickens' work the book will be useful, if at all, only when read consecutively from beginning to end, not excluding the notes. I do not offer rounded or complete discussions of individual novels. As we know, there are very many such excellent discussions available. My essay may best be read as an argument about Dickens' oeuvre in chronological order. It is also, in an important sense, a personal essay, and in the Introduction I offer an elaboration of that point.

Throughout my essay I speak to fellow critics, believing their work to have been indispensable. In an unavoidable way, a book on a major writer cannot but also be a book about the critical thought surrounding him or her. If I take issue here or there it is with a view to furthering the parameters of discussion. I owe a debt to all Dickens' critics, as well as to all other participants in the culture of criticism.

Unless otherwise indicated, I use the Penguin text of Dickens' novels. Acronyms of journals, wherever used, follow the MLA pattern.

Acknowledgments

I would like to thank the Fulbright Foundation in New Delhi, India, for the opportunity provided me to travel to the States and write a final draft of this book. I am particularly grateful to Mr. K. S. Nair for his unfailing helpfulness. I want also to thank Principal Narinder Singh Pradhan and the governing body of Kirori Mal College, University of Delhi, for granting me a leave of absence that brought me to the University of Wisconsin–Madison as a Fulbright Fellow.

My debts to Professor Joseph Wiesenfarth, the present chairman of the Department of English at the University of Wisconsin–Madison, are numerous. I can hardly thank him adequately for finding time to read closely the drafts of my manuscript and for the many suggestions he made concerning it. In addition, he and his wife, Louise, and their son, Adam, welcomed me to their home frequently; and I thank them especially for making my Thursday evenings there truly memorable. I am indebted also to Professor Phillip Herring and his wife, Lydia, for their kind attentions during my stay. Professor Betsy Draine proved a generous and sure resort for books to be had nowhere else, and I thank her for her graciousness to someone whom, to begin with, she knew very slightly.

My friends Carl and Catherine Rasmussen and Donald Itkin together provided me with lodging—indeed, with a home—for five long months and enabled me to give all my time to work. I can truly never thank them enough. They are first among a family of friends—among whom I want also to mention with affection Larry Flescher—who make America a joyful place for me to visit.

I am pleased to record my debt to Professor Nandlal Gupta for having kept me going with his quiet warmth and wisdom. My many discussions with Professor Om Prakash Grewal of Kurukshetra University over many years have had a special place in my education. I am indebted to Dr. Kum Kum Sangari of Inderprastha College, University of Delhi, for sustaining me intellectually at a time when I especially needed enlightened support. Her reading of the first draft of this book resulted in many happy transformations of idiom. I am grateful to Professors Sarup Singh and A. N. Kaul for their encouragement, and to Professor Vinod Sena and Dr. Rani Ray for their felt and friendly concern. To my students at Delhi—many of them now teachers themselves— who stimulated me when everything else failed, I owe very special thanks.

My debt to my wife, Shashi, is very far from a customary one. I can conceive of no worthwhile effort without her; at the same time I fully realize that she has given me too much of herself. Her companionship has enacted for me an intimate meaning for the word *generosity*. The same is true for my son, Ajay, who showed me the most touching consideration in urging me to go abroad at a time when he could least afford my absence. His devotion is equally unforgettable.

I want finally to express my appreciation to Allen Fitchen, director of the University of Wisconsin Press. That he had the patience to read through a rough draft of this book and support its rewriting in its present form is a tribute to his commitment to scholarship and an act of goodwill that one scholar, certainly, will long remember.

Although family members and friends whom I mention here—as well as so many others whom space does not allow me to name—

have actively supported the writing of this book directly and indirectly, they are not of course responsible for any of its shortcomings. These I claim for myself alone.

Madison, Wisconsin
January 1985

Dickens and the Dialectic of Growth

CHAPTER 1

Introduction

I

Thanks to the perceptive critical attention given Dickens over the last four decades (since Edmund Wilson's seminal essay),[1] Henry James's high-minded dismissal has in turn long been duly dismissed.[2] As we know, even Dr. Leavis changed his mind. That he could rise above the particular ideology that obliged him to disregard all of Dickens with the understandable exception of *Hard Times* is a tribute to the persistence of his critical engagements.[3] Dickens scholarship today is a copious industry, and one need have a good reason to add to it. A more severe predicament, however, is created by the unsettled critical climate of the moment. If arbitrary signifiers are hopelessly and forever chasing illusive and nonexistent signifieds then, indeed, as Eagleton suggests, "criticism may be a crippled discourse."[4] And yet, those who still regard critical activity, if one likes the business of *making sense*, as a precondition of human existence as it has been known for some time now can neither simply sulk nor remain complacently aloof.[5] In proportion to the extremity both of the alterations we are being asked to make in our habits of reading and of our evaluatory *Angst*, it is necessary to relocate ourselves in the critical field. And much of this relocation has to be in the field of theory.

As I set out to offer a view of Dickens, I therefore feel the need to place myself among the contending critical counters. These days it is hopeless to imagine that we shall not be found out. Although the debate about theory interests me autonomously in its fullness and although I feel drawn to it, I do not propose to engage in theoretical debate here beyond creating recognizable critical space to allow me to carry on with Dickens. Let me then say a few things rather directly.

The outer anarchic limits of the critic's new-found euphoria at his release from mere secondariness, his boyish delight at what he construes as his delivery from the old-fashioned tyranny of meanings, are expressed nicely by Stanley Fish: "No longer is the critic the humble servant of texts whose glories exist independently of anything he might do." Interpretation is no longer the "art of construing but the art of constructing," and "interpreters do not decode [texts]; they make them."[6] On the face of it Fish's position must seem too self-consciously extreme to warrant a close response; but insofar as it expresses not just an *outré* proposition but a distinct political ideology, it will not do merely to disregard Fish. In the first place, as Robert Scholes points out, there is a difference between "making a poem from a text" and "making a text"; a "page of *Paradise Lost* and a Rorschach blot" are not interchangeable as texts. As long as a text is bound to its language and exists only through it, the probabilities of what we may do *to* it or *with* it are limited in accordance with the ways in which language — every particular language — functions, whether synchronically, diachronically, or both. Fish believes, for example, that the "English language and Christian typology" are the same thing; Scholes correctly points out that a Christian reader without any English is not likely to make much of *Samson Agonistes*.[7] So that what freedom we have is bounded by the rules of the game — be it language or chess (which Barthes and Lévi-Strauss would also call a language) — and what moves we make must implicitly confine themselves to the agreed motions. Of course, the rules can and always do change as a new power-set or a new ideology is in place, but it is self-evident that there can only be new rules and new codes.[8]

It is useful to remember that in revising, indeed rejecting, the notion that the Neogrammarians held of language (as the Kantian "object" of knowledge to be described in its forms and elements), Ferdinand de Saussure redefined language as a system of *relations* as well as "a *social* product . . . and a collection of necessary conventions that have been adopted by a social body to permit individuals" to make meaningful interchange.[9] And when de Saussure speaks of the arbitrary nature of the signifier within a linguistic sign-system, he by no means suggests that the arbitrariness is impenetrably absolute, because within any given culture signifiers are recognizably fixed at various synchronic stages in a process of ongoing diachrony and mutation. Were this not the case human cultures would not only be unsupportable but perhaps unthinkable as well. It is hardly a wonder, therefore, that this functional historicity of the sign-system is fully admitted and held primary by Jacques Derrida, who has widely been credited with having created the current storm by carrying de Saussure's deconstruction of the signifier to the very signified. Derrida writes: "We cannot do without the concept of a sign, we cannot renounce the metaphysical complicity involved in it without at the same moment renouncing the very work of criticism we are directing against it."[10] This is not merely a tactical admission; with characteristic integrity, Derrida is here enunciating the frustrating paradox of his own enterprise: his discourse against discourse is always itself discourse, made possible by the very sign-system that he seeks to demolish. In denying signifieds he is constantly pointing to them as his stream of concepts, nouns and pronouns; and in denying the possibility of meanings, he is at once making ever more sophisticated approximations to fresh meanings: "We have no language — no syntax and no lexicon — which is alien to this history [of Presence]; we cannot utter a single destructive proposition which has not already slipped into the form, the logic, and the implicit postulations of precisely what it seeks to contest." When questioned explicitly as to the procedure which might allow the "I"-center (the subject employing language) to be denied being so long as language is informed by intention, Derrida is again explicit: "I didn't say there was no center; that we could get along without the center," or that "we could get along without the notion of a subject."[11] Derrida, then, presents language as feeling "its way gropingly along the walls of its own conceptual prison, describing it from the inside" without any "illusion of having passed beyond the metaphysics of which it stands as a critique."[12]

The deconstructive position at present may then be formulated thus: first, after Nietzsche, all myths of origin, all ontologies, are mere bad faith, because there is no transcendent subject; second, not only are signifiers arbitrary but the signifieds they are signs of are equally indeterminate. Thus within language or writing (*écriture*) there is only a stream of texuality holding no teleological promise of reachable truths *out there*. In effect, all objectivity is equally problematic and perhaps fake as well. What then *is* left? The individual subject, in a new reversion to the Cartesian cogito (I *write* therefore I am), because, as Julia Kristeva correctly states, "a certain subject is present from the moment that there is the consciousness of a meaning."[13] Every truth claim is false; nevertheless, the truth claim of existential being remains assumed and without question. It is a conundrum: having renounced metaphysics, Derrida has no equipment left to dismantle his own self, or the notion of the self, and he knows it as a painful contradiction. But his followers, in the meanwhile, happily trot along to make assertions that no assertions can be made, to evade reality on the ground that language is groundless and undecidable, while they also go on to reevaluate previous positions and traditions producing the decisive hermeneutic.[14]

Conceding the reality of the perceiving subject (as signifier and signified) in a world bereft of the metaphysical option, Derrida then also accepts the reality of historicity, which is the only way open to the deconstructionist to get at the subject in the absence of metaphysics: "The question [is] of knowing where [the subject] comes from and how it functions."[15] And in what must seem at this point a curious marriage of convenience, Frederic Jameson concurs with Derrida, introducing simultaneously an all-important slide: "We . . . propose the following revised formulation: that history is *not* a text, not a narrative, master or otherwise, but that as an absent cause, it is inaccessible to us except in textual form, and that our approach to it and to the Real itself necessarily passes through its prior texualization, its narrativization in the political unconscious."[16] To Jameson texuality has the potential of a teleology, of making the "political unconscious" conscious in history, and, furthermore, of providing an object, a "Real," to the movement of an unfolding consciousness. Jameson's "absent cause" is, after all, the Spirit's dialectic working through time. This is in clear contrast to the views of Frank Kermode, who finds the whole hermeneutical problematic a bit too much and sees a slide back into metaphysics as rather the only tired romantic option: "The pleasures of interpretation are henceforth linked to loss and disappointment, so that most of us will find the task too hard, or simply repugnant; and then, abandoning meaning, we slip back into transparency, the single sense, the truth," the so-called transparency that Paul de Man questions in his reconsideration of the Romantic symbol.[17] In any case, our obligation, I think, remains that of going on "formulating . . . fresh propositions,"[18] for, quite simply, "there is too much at stake."[19]

In the position we take regarding language we concomitantly declare a politics and an ideology. For a person from the Third World, such as the present writer, to declare a general skepticism about reality based upon the tenuous nature of linguistic signifieds is to immediately announce a stance of reaction. Hungry and sick populations must remain a fairly unmistakable text, and to the extent that such is the case, language has important uses. When Jameson, therefore, argues for the "priority of the political interpretation of literary texts,"[20] he strikes a note that one recognizes as the note of metahistorical necessity. It is a critical-theoretical placement that enables us to ask what combination of social forces should have led to the personal-anarchic subjectivism of the extreme poststructuralist formulations. And it enables us to speculate whether "free play" may not, after all, be the extreme expression within the "Ideological State Apparatus"[21] in the contemporary West of an increasing insistence on "free marketism" in the infrastructure of Western economies. And not at all facetiously. Is it possible that Paul de Man's own comment on the French criticism of 1966 applies here: "Actual institutional and economic interests are involved. There is more at stake than a turnover of generations"?[22] Poststructuralism, as in Derrida, does well to seek to liberate knowledge from resisting ontologies and the fever of final endings, yet the space in between constitutes lived history, which can hardly be deconstructed out of existence. Human misery neither deserves nor brooks maps of misreading.

I prefer therefore deconstructive activity as it has always been used, not just by demythologizing critics, but by acutely self-doubting writers themselves. In that formulation I of course revert to the old-fashioned discrimination between the primary text and its decoding agent, the critic, always allowing that the best criticism is creative and the best creation critical in the finest sense. I see Shakespeare's whole work as a monumental achievement of internal as well as historical deconstruction; I see the odes of Keats as a fine instance in poetry of the consecutive demolition of antecedent assumptions about the nature of reality and the nature of selfhood; and *Tristram Shandy*, *Vanity Fair*, and a whole host of more self-conscious twentieth-century fiction as works constantly alert to and creatively suspicious of the forms and structures that they build from chapter to chapter or textuality to textuality. And quite in that sense I see Dickens' work from the 1830s to the 1860s as one composite *Bildungsroman* that builds progressively superior insights as each succeeding novel deconstructs its predecessor(s) into a mounting historical graph. In current idiom, "all [Dickens'] writing takes place in the light of [his] other writing,"[23] and each new endeavor constitutes an illuminating "molestation"[24] of a previously presented configuration. Dickens also both creates genres and parodies them in creative acts of subversion quite in the sense in which Bakhtin sees the progressive history of "novelization" from the Greeks to Dostoevsky.[25] But that is material for a separate discussion altogether.

II

The present essay sets itself a narrowly specific objective; it seeks to define and demonstrate the quality and scope of movement within the "ideological field"[26] constituted by Dickens' oeuvre. The point of the limited exegeses I offer is to bring into focus the "prior historical or ideological *subtext*"[27] which runs through the abundance of Dickens' presentations. I think it is possible to trace Dickens' career through the subtle and shifting relation between subjective and cultural pressure by following the plotted fates of a series of surrogates in the novels. My contention is that "the true life of the novels," far from being "in the nooks and peripheries" of Dickens' plots, is essentially, though paradoxically, present in the very "blankly absent centre[s]" that Eagleton complains of.[28] Dickens' problematic "centre[s]"—from *Oliver Twist* to *Our Mutual Friend*—suggest in their incremental enactments the novelist's sustained and historically illuminating struggle to come to grips with himself and with the Victorian *Zeitgeist*. The fascination of that struggle is contained in the graduated advances of perception and concomitant art that the novels reveal in time. Dickens' preparedness, however painful, to revise configurations in order to overcome trauma is impressive. It is tempting to observe in passing that whereas the novelists who, we have been told, constitute the "great tradition" of English fiction use irony chiefly as device (remaining essentially unquestioning of quietly assumed certitudes about such categories as morality, intelligence, property, and culture),[29] Dickens, like Dostoevsky, seems truly the novelist driven by an ironic vision. As he dismantles in the fifties and sixties the assumptions that he dearly needed in the decades of the thirties and the forties, Dickens knows the myths of his later work to be residual and fictive. Appropriately, Dickens' endings become progressively either problematic or untenable in ways that are subversive of complacent artistic closure—one might say such closure as would be favored by a middle-class ideology.

When I speak of the movement *within* the ideological field described by Dickens' work I do so advisedly: there can hardly be serious controversy as to the conclusions Dickens arrives at around 1865. My emphasis will be a good deal on the manner in which we approach Dickens' fictions or in which we define the contours of his evaluation of personal and historical reality as he develops from self-extenuation to self-scrutiny. This for the reason that the creatively augmenting relationship between self-awareness and totalizing art in Dickens has yet to receive the sort of strenuously focused attention that can facilitate an understanding of the operative dialectic within his oeuvre. Günter Buck contends that "hermeneutical consciousness cannot catch itself in its own act and thereby reflect itself out of its own historical situation";[30] I think we can show that this does happen in Dickens, that it is not only we, the critics after the fact, who now know that Dickens develops but that the Dickens dialectic is internal evidence of Dickens catching himself in each repeated act at a higher point of clarification. In using the term *dialectic* I mean a fairly straight-forward reference to its classic formulation in Hegel, whose term *Aufhebung* captures the essence of its dynamics—the concept of how the negative, that which is being negated in the dialectical process, is at once superseded and preserved.[31] Dickens' novels re-turn with ever-increasing rigor to the one central contradiction of his career, that which involves his simultaneous roles as aspiring, successful, and disgusted Victorian. And this creative opposition of antithetical drives can be isolated from *Oliver Twist* onwards with a consistency sufficient enough to possess the force of a valid generalization. I see the initial point of the Dickens dialectic pro-jected in the opposition between, on the one hand, Dick and the early Oliver and, on the other hand, Dick and the later Oliver. And the overall scope of this dialectic stretches, I argue, across the subtly evolving modalities of social vision and art that carry Dickens from Oliver to Charley Hexam—indeed, that *transform* Oliver into Charley Hexam.

An important critical motivation of my reading is also, then, to offer a corrective to the overkill of influential culture-criticism of Dickens, both of the Marxist and the bourgeois variety. Such criticism has tended to oversimplify Dickens' motivations as a so-cial critic; it is my view that this oversimplification results from our failure to respond to the dialectical tension of Dickens' art. The linear premises of that old debate between Jackson and Or-well continue to bedevil an integrated and objective perception of Dickens' ideological problematic. Jackson and Orwell both ignore the complex working-out of the politics of Dickens' fictions be-cause both, in writing abstractly of Dickens' ideology, seek at bottom only an affirmation of their own. I think it worthwhile to resurrect the essentials of that old debate even at the risk of seeming archaic because the intervening historical criticism of Dickens has not advanced us qualitatively beyond those positions, or beyond those positions *as* methodologies.

Jackson postulates, we recall, that Dickens' "radicalism . . .

might easily have emerged as positive Socialism or Communism."[32] In this attempt, in Orwell's phrase, to steal Dickens for communism,[33] Jackson expectedly runs into intractable problems, ironically in the very novels which appeal to him by virtue of their seemingly revolutionary content—*Barnaby Rudge, A Tale of Two Cities*, and *Hard Times*. Clearly, he is either unable or unwilling to make the distinction between revolutionary novels and novels about revolution. Dismayed by the way Dickens treats the rioters in *Barnaby Rudge* (insofar as they may be viewed as analogues for the Chartists), Jackson cannot acquit Dickens "of concocting a burlesque of the 'underground' Radical clubs . . . and of the trade unions of the period before the repeal of the Combination Acts in 1825," nor can he understand why "Dickens does not seem to have been . . . at all disposed to join with, or to champion . . . the Chartists."[34] Likewise, he finds "wrong from beginning to end" Dickens' presentation of trade unionism in *Hard Times* and blames the distortion on Carlyle. Jackson simply assumes that "Dickens always thought of himself as one of the common people,"[35] whereas we know that until well after his first child could speak, Dickens had not forgiven his parents for having obliged him to work in Warrens' blacking house "with common men and boys."[36] Jackson quotes confidently from a letter Dickens wrote Forster in March 1844, in which Dickens speaks of the sad condition of English society and prognosticates that "the more I see of its extraordinary conceit, and its stupendous ignorance of what is passing out of doors, the more certain I am that it is approaching the period when being incapable of reforming itself it will have to submit to being reformed by others off the face of the earth."[37] Characteristically, Jackson reads this as Dickens' hope for revolution. Dickens' emphasis on the failure of "society" is obvious; but what is equally obvious is that in the prospect of its correction by "others" Dickens expresses, not hope, but apocalyptic panic ("off the face of this earth"). The opposition Dickens builds here between "society" and the "others" is of course immediately revealing of his ideological problematic, and Raymond Williams has shown us brilliantly how that dichotomy strikes at the heart of conservative-liberal attitudes of the middle nineteenth century.[38] Dickens' stance in this letter is parallel with Carlyle's reconstruction of the French Revolution: both are in effect saying that should reform fail (self-serving reform, one might add) the inevitable must happen in England as it did in France. And we know, of course, that Dickens defined himself as "a Reformist heart and soul."[39] When one recaptures this correspondence of attitudes between Dickens and Carlyle, one is hardly surprised that the two men were on the same side of the Eyre controversy of 1865, both supporting the exoneration of the British officer who had cavalierly ordered the execution of five hundred black people in Jamaica.[40]

If Jackson shoots wholly one way, Orwell shoots the other. He asserts that there is nothing "socialistic" about Dickens; ostensibly, throughout his career Dickens asks only that "capitalists ought to be kind, not that workers ought to be rebellious." Orwell believes that until the very end Dickens is only "vaguely on the side of the working class," and that he was at bottom quite simply "a nineteenth-century liberal."[41] Jackson reads the fragment of autobiography which Dickens sent Forster (sometime between 1847 and 1848) and draws the most unsupportable conclusions from it. Orwell infers from Bechhofer Robert's fictional-biographical attack on Dickens, *On This Side Idolatry*, that "a writer's literary personalilty has little or nothing to do with his private character"—which does not prevent him from misreading Pip's attitude towards Magwitch as "obviously the attitude of Dickens himself."[42] Taken separately, Jackson's and Orwell's views (and the corresponding lines of analysis descending from them) prove inadequate in exploring the totality of diverging tensions within Dickens' lived art. Yet, taken together, they help to establish for us Dickens' problematical though creative ambivalence in his relation to his culture. That the problem Dickens works out over thirty years of writing is more steadfastly akin to Orwell's own problem is underscored by Raymond Williams in an acute comment on *Writers and Leviathan*: "What is being recorded, in Orwell, is the experience of . . . a man who, while rejecting the consequences of an atomist society, yet retains deeply, in himself, its characteristic mode of consciousness."[43] Williams' critique includes George Eliot, Matthew Arnold, and the John Stuart Mill of "On Liberty," all of whom, in seeking to evaluate the available culture as object, ignore or conceal their own direct and vital relationship to that culture.[44]

The crucial fact about Dickens is that he both urgently aspired to the substantive fruits of the bourgeois culture that surrounded him and intensely despised the living expressions of bourgeois Victorian insensitivity. The forces which had placed Dickens, along with others far worse off than he, in the blacking factory and had unforgivably outraged and scarred him were also the forces that Dickens sought to make his own. The movement of Dickens' consciousness within the problematic of this contradiction is also the movement within his art. Its dynamics are related to the growing clarity and acceptance with which Dickens dramatizes this division in the structures of his fiction. The structural strategies of *Oliver Twist* plainly suggest his frightened awareness of the contradiction. The early and the late fiction are defined by the varying degrees of emancipation with which he allows himself to approach this contradiction.

III

The dialectic of experience in Dickens, then, is rooted in a complex structure of feeling and deeply embedded in the famous blacking-factory trauma of his boyhood — always square one in school stories about Dickens, or rather about Copperfield. I want, nonetheless, to return to that *cause célèbre* of Dickens' life in order to see how we might make critically profitable inferences from it and base our entry into *Oliver Twist* within its evident self-divisions. It is not my intention to make out of the blacking factory an origin or an ontology, but to proceed much in the spirit of establishing, as Althusser says, "the recognition of the givenness of the complex structure . . . which governs the . . . development" of our knowledge of any reality, what he succinctly nominates as "déjà-donnée" or pre-givenness.[45] Dickens criticism has made meager use of that experience in reading the forms of his novels. In taking a closer look at Dickens' articulation of that experience in the autobiography he sent Forster, my purpose is to formulate the energy and the shape of the contradiction that generates Dickens' sustained self-exploration.

The moving urgency of the fragment of autobiography[46] — which Dickens wrote sometime in 1847, just before his first use of the

first-person narrative form in *David Copperfield* — issues from two
defining perceptions: first, Dickens' insistently exclusive valuation
of himself and his corresponding hurt at not having been thought
to deserve better; second, his submerged but noticeable awareness that perhaps some guilt attached to his whole attitude toward himself. The real edge of his suffering did not lie so much
in the physical deprivation of his condition as in the inference that
perhaps his lot, after all, might be thought too easily comparable
with that of Bob Fagin or Poll Green or Mealy Potatoes. The ac-
cusations that Dickens levelled against his parents, his mother in
particular — "I never afterwards forgot, I never shall forget, I never
can forget, that my mother was warm for my being sent back" —
did not derive from the actual fact that they obliged him to work
for a living but from his sense that in obliging him to work in
that place and with *those* people they had shown themselves hei-
nously oblivious and disregardful of his extraordinary merits.
Thus, Dickens writes, "It is wonderful to me that even after my
descent into the poor little drudge I had been since I came to London, no one had compassion enough on me — a child of *singular
abilities*: quick, eager, delicate, and soon hurt, bodily or men-
tally."[47] That Dickens can write of himself in these terms as late
as 1847 without any apparent embarrassment testifies to the critical importance of the question of *distance* in an evaluation of
Dickens' career. Almost to the end what occupies Dickens' art is
a tension between what Althusser calls "ideology" and "knowledge" (defined as critical distance from ideology).[48] Again: "No
words can express the secret agony of my soul as I sunk into this
companionship . . . and felt my early hopes of growing up to be
a learned and distinguished man crushed in my breast"; unbear-
able was "the shame that I felt in my position," having to work
"from morning to night, with common men and boys, a shabby
child." The fact is that the autobiographical piece — written as late,
I emphasize, as 1847 — is an intensely class-conscious document.
Dickens' exceptionally strong and felt impulse towards "differentiation" is ironically revealed, furthermore, even in the nature of
his consolations in the blacking house.[49]

In one way his companions in the warehouse, co-sufferers though
they were, became the source of Dickens' agony; and yet, in an-

other way, looking at them he knew he was different and superior: "Though . . . familiar with them, my conduct and manners were different from theirs to place a space between us," and they would "treat me as one upon a different footing from the rest" and "always spoke of me as "the young gentleman." (Between this statement and Pip's corrective confession is a period of fifteen years.) Dickens' anxiety on this score was so deeply felt that on one occasion, when young Charles was seized with a disorder, Bob Fagin offered to take him home "under his protection"; however, Dickens writes, "I was too proud to let him know about the prison; and after making several efforts to get rid of him, to all of which Bob Fagin in his goodness was deaf, shook hands with him on the steps of a house . . . making believe that I lived there." This resentment of Fagin's conciliatory "goodness" translates into evil in the Fagin of *Oliver Twist*; good and evil alike threaten to assimilate the ambitious boy. Yet, Dickens' perception of Bob Fagin's "goodness" is fraught with guilt, as is his excessively self-regarding response to the award of a Royal Academy prize to his favorite sister Fanny. Dickens writes: "I could not bear to think of myself — beyond the reach of all such emulation and success. The tears ran down my face. I felt as if my heart were rent. I prayed, when I went to bed that night, to be lifted out of the humiliation and neglect in which I was. I never had suffered so much before. There was no envy in this." It does, of course, occur to Dickens that there might be "envy in this." Likewise, the parents Dickens held responsible for his humiliation and what seemed his lost destiny were sadly missed at the end of the day when he would go "home to such a miserable blank," being "so cut off from my parents, my brothers, and sister." We think of the crowded families in Dickens who may not have much but who are happy in each other (the Toodles in *Dombey and Son* or the legendary Cratchits in *A Christmas Carol*).[50]

The autobiographical fragment, then, fully reveals a complex and internally opposed structure of feeling, comprising (1) an obsessive sense of personal destiny and a corresponding need of success; (2) a precious sense of great personal vulnerability ("I was so young and childish, and so little qualified — how could I be otherwise? — to undertake the whole charge of my existence"), bordering frequently on panic and entailing a pervasive plea for protection; (3) a faintly felt sense of guilt, suggested in Dickens' pique at Bob Fagin's "goodness," at Fanny's success, and in the strength of his resentment against his parents; and (4) an incipient sense (eventually as a "subtext") that the twofold desire for sympathy and success contained within itself the seed of a far-reaching contradiction, necessitating, at some point, the declaration of a clearly perceived historical allegiance. And it is this complex structure of feeling which constitutes the operative dynamics of Dickens' fiction from the early to the late.

I suggest that the developing interiority of this structure, its developing resolution, is best understood by examining the adjustment that Dickens makes to a composite self-image in the fiction. This self-image comprises, for purposes of this discussion, Oliver, Dick, and the Dodger in *Oliver Twist*; Nicholas and Smike in *Nicholas Nickleby*; Little Nell and Kit Nubbles in *The Old Curiosity Shop*; Paul, Florence, and Walter Gay in *Dombey and Son*; young Martin in *Martin Chuzzlewit*; David, Steerforth, and Traddles in *David Copperfield*; Pip and Herbert Pocket in *Great Expectations*; and Charley Hexam in *Our Mutual Friend*. Although I do not offer separate discussions of *Bleak House, Hard Times, Little Dorrit*, and *A Tale of Two Cities*, I do suggest where Esther, Louisa, Amy, and Arthur belong in Dickens' career as I see it, as well as the nature of Dickens' attempt and achievement in those novels. Of course, I do not include all Dickens' writing, nor do I feel overly anxious about not doing so. As I said at the outset, the validity of a critical reading is hardly incumbent upon mechanical or quantum totalization. What is important is that a reading be sufficiently valid as a generalization — a generalization that can hold as an argument. I approach such a generalization by establishing, contrary to the views of Orwell and other readers, that Dickens does dramatize in his novels a "process" that has intimate and extensive meaning for the nineteenth century.[51] It may be true that characters often do not develop within a single Dickens novel (living in "worlds" of their own);[52] "process" in Dickens stretches across the whole body of his work, and it is that critical movement I seek to isolate. That my procedure runs the risk of being exclusive or reductive of Dickens' total production I am aware.

Yet, I am also aware that therein I share a not uncommon critical fate. Is it not always the case that a major writer, a "classic," possesses "a surplus adequate to accommodate more than one interpreter and more than any one generation of interpreters"?[53]

IV

What I say above is obviously narrow in limiting Dickens' relevance to the nineteenth century. In the Preface I stated that this book is also a personal book, a required discovery. The manner in which Dickens came to have interest for me may also substantiate the peculiar relevance of his career to thinking people throughout the Third World today. In deconstructing Dickens I deconstruct myself in a way that has been of profit to me and may perhaps be of profit to a few others in a like historical predicament. If what follows reads like a page from a history text, it is well to remember that the new theorists I spoke of at the outset have taught us that the boundaries between "disciplines" are after all not only elusive but often unreal. They have also taught us that literary production has no special privilege and that it is "production" like any other production, although its field is such that many different varieties of production intersect within it.[54] The important thing is that we are able to make sensible and historically illuminating statements about all this production—which is exactly the point at which our mentors of today desert us. But we can only go on trying to make sense without the illusion that disputes as to what constitutes legitimate territory can be resolved in the foreseeable critical future—or ever at all. There is no end to jostling and rubbing of elbows. It is all that we have for the moment.

For those of us who live in the "developing" world the years since the end of the Second World War have been momentous. India obtained independence from British colonial rule in 1947 and, as a nation state, launched on planned economic development (within a liberal-democratic framework) along socialistic lines. As years went by, a powerful national bourgeoisie (limited to the state and twenty-odd "houses") succeeded in establishing a strong industrial base. Within thirty years food production doubled; the coal, steel, oil, cement, and communications industries achieved vast expansion, as did education. Yet, distressingly, disparities in purchasing power increased with equal rapidity, making constitutional guarantees of equal opportunity for all citizens increasingly an unrealizable abstraction. The distribution of goods and services — only goods, really, since service is still a nonexistent concept — became selectively strangulated; hordes of dispossessed laborers migrated from villages to sprawling urban centers; slums sprang up everywhere in metropolitan areas; and often, despite stored stocks of food, grain prices shot up. The hoarding of commodities for sale in a flourishingly lucrative black market became preponderant (paralleling in circulation of total wealth the revenues of the government of India). The starkness of famine gave way to a more insidious deprivation, namely malnutrition. All this in the middle of ever more sophisticated advances both in industrial and agricultural technology, nuclear and even space research. Today India ranks tenth among industrial nations and has the third most numerous working force of scientists and technologists in the world, yet the "two nations" remain as I have outlined them.

To those of us who were acquainted with the advent of modern industrialism in England (from the first railway in 1830) and with the subsequent story of English "development," it seemed that in every significant respect we in India were reenacting the hard ambition and optimism as well as the accompanying callousness and the widespread social tragedy of that era in England. After pushing out the British, an affluent national bourgeoisie became colonizers. A special trauma was reserved for those of us who grew up semiprivileged but radical in the decade after independence: we discovered that we had become supereducated and well-to-do (in contrast to eight out of ten Indians who were illiterate and living below thinkable levels of subsistence). Soon, the egalitarian jargon we mouthed deceived nobody, not even ourselves.

In a world that we continue to see as hypocritical and unjust, it has been difficult to place ourselves (unless among the privileged class), to define our *loci*. And for those of us who went on to become teachers, the search for perspectives has been often agonizing, more especially if we happened to be teachers of an alien literary tradition. It was in the context of this sort of introspection that Dickens acquired for me over the years the force of a kindred recognition. Of the major intelligences engaged with the Victorian scene, Dickens, placed as he was, seemed the most closely to approximate the ambition, the self-doubt, and the guilt of many of us in India, who, as I said, had begun well but ended well-to-do. His career as a socially engaged artist carried a special meaning, as one saw him relocating himself from novel to novel. And it became important to try to understand how he perhaps saw himself in the developing critique of his novels.

I did not find a study of Dickens that argued for or demonstrated *necessary* continuities between the early Dickens and the late. And if I was right about a process of sustained introspection within Dickens, then such continuities had, in a sense, to be present. In a book which I think indispensable, Monroe Engel wrote: "I am interested to show the increasing extent to which Dickens became a conscious artist, and this interest is served more clearly by the later novels than by his fiction of the thirties and the forties."[55] Engel's book, however, makes it a fair inference that his interest is in showing that the later novels are better art than the earlier, rather than in isolating bases which can help connect the early and the late in a historically illuminating way. Similarly, another valuable book posits that "we must face the fact that at the beginning of his career, Dickens' imagination contained elements of vulgarity and sentimentality, in common with those of his age."[56] This may well be true, but the presence of vulgarity and sentimentality is not accounted for with the sort of attention that can make the art available to us as something revealing. It remains merely a statement. A more recent work assumes that if one is interested in "texts as literary experiences" then one's study "is inevitably aesthetic rather than sociological."[57] My own view here is that the dichotomy we set up between the "aesthetic" and the "sociological" is false and reflective in itself of a particular kind of social thinking. At any rate, my own argument about Dickens is that the forms of his novels (their aesthetic) are throughout closely implicated in the scope of his social thinking, and I seek to suggest precisely how we can see this necessary unity in the novels from the thirties to the sixties. Even a sophisticated social critic like Eagleton makes an unhelpful nondialectical summation: "The early Dickens' perception of character as idiosyncratic and nonrelational" does not lead "to a vision of social unity."[58] The pattern persists: early bad, late good. It can hardly be my contention that the later Dickens is not the more considerable Dickens; that would be reckless. That many of us still enjoy the early work is of course beside the point. If, however, we can show how the achievement of the later novels is contingent upon a process of continuing personal and cultural evaluation by the novelist, a process analyzable in terms of the strategies of his art, we may acquire a more integrated sense of Dickens' total effort.

Finally, I am aware that what I seek to do is perhaps critically old-fashioned. A sampling of Dickens criticism of the last decade will show how our attention has been drawn to such matters as Dickens' imagination, his language, his rhetoric, his comedy, his violence, his energy, his excess. That is a pretty colorful harvest, and titles and authors will spring to mind at the categories I mention. It is also true that Hegelian approaches find disfavor with the existentialist, the visionary, and the reader who sees literature as pure object or as genre. Likewise, those who prefer spatiality, design, architectonics, or myth as critical ideologies, or those others who espouse the joy of fictiveness, fantasy, and the carnivalesque will find tedious the enumeration of "growth"; others might contend that "ideals of development form a central aspect of our mythic apparatus, where they reinforce a strongly individualist ideology."[59] I seek, nevertheless, to recover for myself and for like-minded readers what seems to me something essential in the way Dickens saw himself and his culture, to show, by a study of kinetic images, Dickens thinking his art towards greater, more divining intelligence, and to suggest that an understanding of an "individualist ideology" can, if we are willing, yield rich social dividends.

CHAPTER 2

Oliver Twist:
The Critical Problem

I

In 1951 Arnold Kettle spoke of the "struggle throughout *Oliver Twist* between the plot and the pattern." Kettle defined "pattern" in the novel as the "struggle of the poor against the bourgeois state," and located its resonant center in the gruel scene. As for the plot, Kettle argued that "the plot and Brownlow emerge in the novel at the same moment, for their purpose is identical": the plot and Mr. Brownlow together rescue Oliver from the underworld and "establish him as a respectable member of society."[1] Subsequent readings of *Oliver Twist* have had to contend with Kettle's forceful—perhaps definitive—analysis. There are of course readings that have provided acute textual exegeses of the inner atmosphere of the novel, of the quality of the relation between patterns of image and areas of emotional and psychological concentration— readings which have greatly enhanced our appreciation of the sources of the power that Dickens' writing exerts upon us. Of these Hillis Miller's study is still perhaps the most outstanding.[2] Yet no reading, as far as I know, which has sought to address the problematic question of Oliver himself—the critical question of what

Eagleton called the "blank centre" — has attempted to explore the implications of Kettle's thesis for Dickens' total career as social being and as artist.[3] Some have sought, vainly, to wish away the problem; most have talked around it in ingenious but equally vain formal, generic, or mystical terms.

John Bayley's perceptive though uneven essay illustrates the confusion that must result from wishing away the problem. Bayley acknowledges that "*Oliver Twist* is not a satisfying novel — it does not liberate us." Having said this, however, Bayley tells us, with mysterious certitude, that "contradictions are resolved in the imaginative certainty of the novel," since Dickens' "imagination makes nonsense . . . of theories of how human beings will or will not behave in a given environment." Unfortunately, in Bayley's essay "imaginative certainty" remains a nebulous phrase, identifiable, finally, only with the "needs of the plot." Bayley recognizes in passing that "the power of *Oliver Twist* depends more than any other Dickens' novel on his personality and background." Unsuspecting of the contrary or dialectical nature of Dickens' motivation, however, Bayley does not see that not only the "power" but equally the distortions in the novel derive from Dickens' "personality and background." Bayley's fascination with the novel's power prevents him from seeing the creative nature of the novel's failure: he sees the failure but rationalizes it.[4]

Likewise, the critical failure to place the internal imperatives of Dickens' conflicting outlook in *Oliver Twist* within perspectives afforded by his oeuvre has led to peculiarly extraneous species of interpretation. Thus, *Oliver Twist* is made out to be the case of a picaresque gone antipicaresque; it is not suggested why this happens, if it does.[5] Or, it is said that Dickens' novel is at bottom a reworking of folklore and fairytale — Cinderella, Hansel and Gretel, and so on — and needs to be read as such.[6] Most dangerously extraneous, because most facilely metaphysical, is the influential suggestion that the critical problem in the novel resolves itself magically once we see that Oliver is, after all, the "vessel of Grace" and that his speaking the King's English is Dickens' way of conveying to us Oliver's status as one of the elect.[7] This is the sort of high-critical fiat against which one is speechless, although so far as I can make out from Dickens' novel, the only thing that saves Oliver is his "inheritance" (ch. 2). Moreover, the whole thrust of Dickens' sociological assumptions—in the Prefaces and the dramatized social vision of the powerful first quarter of the novel—makes nonsense of uncritical applications of a determinist theology to the workings of his art.[8] If Oliver's poverty (read with his incorruptible innocence) were indeed a sign of his election, there would hardly be the need to engineer a plot to "save" him. We recall that as late as 1843 Dickens wrote to Forster, "It's harder for the poor to be virtuous than for the rich."[9] This is not the utterance of a man who thinks the poor "blessed" because "theirs is the Kingdom of Heaven." *Oliver Twist* demonstrates that Dickens thinks exactly the opposite: one must be rich if virtue is to be preserved. That, in fact, defines the initial state of Dickens' problematic.

Oliver Twist simply remains a dissatisfying piece of work. No hermeneutics, however ingenious, can successfully bring its self-divisions into an assimilated unity; its contradictions are what they are—contradictions. Nevertheless, if one is interested in comprehending the nature of Dickens' overall movement, the contradictions in *Oliver Twist* can be illuminating. Critically, the fruitful thing to do is to understand the social bases of these contradictions. Dickens' uneven achievement in the novel can then be seen in an organic relationship to the quality of adjustment that he is making to the structure of feeling I outlined—from what is in *Oliver Twist* a point of minimal distance. Given that understanding, his failure in *Oliver Twist* appears necessary as well as creative, and it proceeds not simply from the exigencies of serial publication—hasty plotting, audience response, and so forth—but also from a failure deeply and directly embedded in his personal and cultural donnée.[10] Indeed, Dickens' plotting in the novel is the aesthetic expression of a social and moral failure of nerve. *Oliver Twist* presents and defines Dickens' problematic in its most undigested form. It reveals Dickens closest to paranoia, so close that he is obliged to distort his proposed social vision in order to save himself. The strength and also the collapse of his achievement derive equally from a near-total absence of distance from felt urgencies of experience. Its raw sense of menace gives the "evil" its extraordinary, almost archetypal, force, and his hypersensitive, atomistic self-awareness makes the vanquishing of that "evil" an imperative. Hence the "pattern" and "plot" that Kettle speaks of — as a forceful but *self-alienating* indictment of the available power structure, also as a contrived entrance into its mythologized identity.

II

Kincaid wrote in 1968 that *Oliver Twist* "is powerful despite all that Dickens could do to make it conventional and safe . . . it represents a triumph of unconscious forces over conscious intentions."[11] In that statement "conscious intentions" are to be identified with making the novel "conventional and safe," and "unconscious forces" ostensibly are those that give us the best, most persuasively dramatized portions of the novel's action. It is my view that exactly the opposite is true. Dickens' Preface to the Third Edition (of 1841)[12] incorporates his conscious intentions; Dickens tells us that as a serious-minded social realist he finds it a case of ideological bad faith that in the literature before him "allurements and fascinations are thrown around" underworld characters — as in Gay's *Beggar's Opera* — because reality does not support those romanticized and fictitious presentations. Dickens proposes, therefore, to "draw a knot of such associates in crime as *really do exist*; to paint them in all their deformity, in all their wretchedness, in all the squalid poverty of their lives; to show them *as they really are* . . ." (emphasis added). To do so would be "a service to society." Let me quote fully the famous passage:

What manner of life is that which is described in these pages, as the every-day existence of a Thief? What charms has it for the young and ill-disposed, what allurements for the most jolter-headed of juveniles? Here are no canterings upon moonlit heaths, no merrymakings in the snuggest of all possible caverns, none of the attractions of dress, no embroidery, no lace, no jack-boots, no crimson coats and ruffles, none of the dash and freedom with which "the road" has been, time out of mind, invested. The cold, wet, shelterless midnight streets of London; the foul and frowzy dens, where vice is closely packed and lacks the room to turn; the haunts of hunger and disease, the shabby rags that scarcely hold together; where are the attractions of these things?

That, indeed, is a stirring expression of Dickens' "conscious intentions," wherein he seeks to place once and for all, a whole tradition of literary presentation and its informing ideology, the politics of an older form, for what it has been — a fictive, *interested*
falsehood. That Dickens' portrayal of the underworld — as well as
of its analogue in the sanctioned power structure, the workhouse,
and the "gentlemen of the Board" — was thoroughly researched and
shockingly true to life we know from various contemporary accounts of Saffron Hill, Jacob's Island, and other East End slums
of London.[13] And the great power of *Oliver Twist* — contrary to
Kincaid's position — derives precisely from Dickens' ability to enact
his conscious intentions. After Fagin, Sikes, Nancy, Claypole, the
Dodger, Fang, Bumble, and Mrs. Mann, nobody could be innocent about what went on and still expect to be credible. Dickens
had destroyed that innocence at one blow and demythologized
middle-class polemics about crime and criminals, about the allegedly inherent irredeemable ill nature of a whole class of human beings. In effect, Dickens said the following: (1) that thieves
and assorted underworld characters are not figures of enviable
romance but creatures full of "wretchedness" and "misery"; (2) that,
being wretched and miserable, they could hardly be criminals by
volition, for "where are the attractions of these things"; (3) that
if he could get "society" to understand his view of this social question, society might then be induced to make appropriate adjust-
ments, not least for its own good. These positions are consistent
with the strongly held behavioral assumptions of Dickens' sociology as one comes across them in his letters, in his speeches, and
in his writings for *Household Words* and *All the Year Round*. One
of Dickens' persistent convictions was that the quality of environment, in its most physical aspects, determined the general quality
of life. Thus he argues that unless slums were cleared and slum-
dwellers shown "Heaven" first by way of some "light and air" and
a "piece of the sky," it was futile to expect any moral betterment
in their lives.[14] "I have always been convinced," Dickens wrote,
"that this Reform [of slum clearance] must precede all other Social Reforms; that it must prepare the way for Education, even
for Religion; and that without it, those classes of people which

increase the fastest, must become so desperate and be made so miserable, as to bear within themselves the certain seeds of ruin to the whole community" (Preface to the 1858 edition). Dickens' first full enactment of that vision is undertaken as late as *Bleak House*: poor Jo becomes the "seed" that spells "ruin to the whole community."

Dickens' most eloquent and unequivocal expression of the view that human nature is conditioned by environment is contained in his 1851 address to the Metropolitan Sanitary Association (from which I quoted briefly above). Imagining himself as one of the exploited wretches, he asked:

What avails it to send a Missionary to me, a miserable man or woman living in a foetid court where every sense bestowed upon me for my delight becomes a torment, and every minute of my life is new mire added to the heap under which I lie depended? To what natural feeling within me is he to address himself? What ancient chord within me can he hope to touch? . . . Is it a rememberance of distortion and decay, scrofula and fever? Would he address himself to my hopes of immortality? I am so surrounded with filth that my soul cannot rise to the contemplation of an immaterial existence![15]

And yet, in the teeth of everything Dickens has been saying, Oliver is to remain miraculously untouched by the influence — the *necessary* influence, according to Dickens' pronouncements in what I have quoted of him — of "every . . . circumstance" no matter how "adverse" (Preface to the Third Edition); of Oliver we are told that "nature . . . had implanted a good sturdy spirit" in his breast. It is not a criticism of Oliver that he remains, as an individual, "good" to the bitter end; we have all known people whose goodness remains undented by adverse circumstance. Therefore, also, a defense of him (such as Bayley's) on the chance grounds of probability is irrelevant. But there are valid criticisms of Oliver: (1) as a "principle," a theoretical construct, he vitiates the terms of Dickens' sociological assault and makes nonsense of the assumptions that function as Dickens' motivation for writing the novel in the first place; (2) we see nothing of a struggle in defense of Oliver's innocence, but the innocence is protected for him;[16] (3) his goodness has not the slightest dramatic force in the novel; (4) his triumph over evil in the end is denoted eventually by respectable birth and comfortable circumstance — by "inheritance"; (5) his assimilation into an idealized bourgeois paradise is projected, *ipso facto*, as proof of his elect status;[17] (6) the principles and convictions upon which Dickens organizes experience in those portions of the novel which issue from his conscious intentions are neutralized and rendered infructuous by the quality of Oliver's separate and exceptional destiny.

It seems hardly probable, though not inconceivable, that Dickens was unable to perceive the contradiction. If he allowed it so blatantly, then, the motivation lies deeper, in the command of the "unconscious forces." And the unconscious forces do not shape the social vision of the novel: they shape the plot. Dickens' minimal distance from himself and, consequently, his frustrating dichotomy of response to the "society" he sets out to indict make the plot inevitable. "It is very much harder for the poor to be virtuous than it is for the rich": the ruling class and the dehumanized institutions it engenders must be taken to task for what they have done to the poor. Simultaneously, the only hope the poor have of securing "virtue" is by attaining to some ideal state of bourgeois comfort. Thus, the need to fabricate a Brownlow as an agent of and a referent for Oliver's "triumph." Not until *The Old Curiosity Shop* does this formulation about wealth and virtue begin to be suspect. Until *Dombey and Son* Dickens largely eats the cake and has it too.

Further on in the Preface to the Third Edition, Dickens makes a bold enunciation of his position with respect to his middle-class audience. It is a position of critical distance, a self-appointed locus that is calculated to allow objective judgment of society and its codes:

But there are people of so refined and delicate a nature, that they cannot bear the contemplation of these horrors . . . criminal characters, to suit them, must be, like their meat, in delicate disguise. A Massaroni in green velvet is quite an enchanting creature; but a Sikes in fustian is insupportable. A Mrs. Massaroni, being a lady in short petticoats and a fancy dress, is a thing to imitate in tableaux and have in lithograph on pretty songs; but a Nancy, being a creature in a cotton gown and cheap shawl, is not to be thought of. It is wonderful how Virtue turns from dirty stockings; and how Vice, married to ribbons and a little gay attire, changes her name, as wedded ladies do, and becomes Romance.

Now, as the stern and plain truth . . . was . . . the purpose of this book, I will not, for these readers, abate one hole in the Dodger's coat, or one scrap of curl-paper in the girl's dishevelled hair. I have no faith in the delicacy which cannot bear to look upon them. I have no desire to make proselytes among such people. I have no respect for their opinion, good or bad; do not covet their amusement. I venture to say this without reserve; for I am not aware of any writer in our language having a respect for himself, or held in any respect by his posterity, who ever has descended to the taste of this fastidious class.

The critical-ideological enterprise Dickens sets himself here is in its minutiae comparable to the terms of George Bernard Shaw's "Apology" for *Mrs. Warren's Profession*. The "delicacy" (of "this fastidious class") that Dickens derides "without reserve" is also the delicacy that Shaw assaults. Just as Dickens' exposure is inspired by a falsifying literary tradition, so also is Shaw's attack provoked by a dramatic tradition "so flaccid in its sentimentality" that it can be countered only by the "reintroduction" of an "ironwork of fact" (precisely Dickens' contention). Much as the "sanctimonious British public" would like Shaw to "throw the whole guilt of Mrs. Warren's profession on Mrs. Warren herself," the "whole aim" of Shaw's plan "is to throw that guilt on the British public itself." Shaw continues:

Mrs. Warren is not a whit a worse woman than the reputable daughter who cannot endure her. Her indifference to the ultimate social consequences of her means of making money and her discovery of that means by the ordinary method of taking the line of least resistance to getting it, are too common in English society to call for any special remark. Her vitality, her spirit, her energy, her outspokenness . . . and the managing capacity which has enabled her . . . to climb from the fried fish shop down by the mint to the establishment of which she boasts, are all high English social virtues. . . . Mrs. Warren's defense of herself is not only bold . . . but valid and unanswerable. . . . Though it is quite natural and right for Mrs. Warren to choose what is, according to her lights, the least immoral alternative, it is none the less infamous of society to offer such alternatives. For the alternatives offered are not morality and immorality, but two sorts of immorality. The man who cannot see that starvation, over-work, dirt, and disease are immoral as prostitution . . . is . . . a hope-lessly private person.[18]

The parallels are obvious. Dickens and Shaw address themselves to an identical social and moral problem with a view to project-ing the "facts" (Shaw) "as they really are" (Dickens). Both propose to disregard the squeamishness, the "delicacy," of the respectable British middle class in order to call a spade a spade. Shaw's attack on the hypocrisy, the decadence, of the sanctimonious British pub-lic is total, exemplified in Mrs. Warren's refusal to accept guilt or censure for her profession. Her clear-eyed "outspokenness" is in-vested with a moral quality superior to the ethics of society. Shaw, then, takes a trenchantly self-alienating position in relation to the audience he seeks to improve. Now Dickens' position, in what I quoted above, seems similar; only, is it? In the Preface Dickens goes on to say: "No less consulting my own taste, than the man-ners of the age, I endeavoured . . . to banish from the lips of the lowest character I introduced, any expression that could by pos-sibility offend. . . . In the case of [Nancy], in particular, I kept this intention constantly in view." The separation that Dickens places between "my own taste" and "the manners of the age" is, it is painfully obvious, tantamount merely to quibbling. They are one and the same. Where Shaw's Mrs. Warren is given a force of intellect, of ideological clarity, that enables her to see the British middle class as morally inferior to her, Dickens' disabling strategy is to make Nancy only too miserably crippled by her sense of her own status as a moral leper, not good enough for the Maylies and the Brownlows. In banishing bad language from the underworld Dickens valorizes language as hierarchy — as an *endorsed* hierar-chy, just as Oliver's King's English is calculated to produce a "moral disconnection" between him and the thieves' den.[19] One also no-tices how Dickens' characterization at this point proceeds from the depths of unanalyzed instinct: there is no flinching, no quali-fication about that use of "lowest character" in the above quota-tion. The fact of the matter is that Oliver's context is, without mediation, Dickens' own: "My conduct and manners," Dickens wrote Forster, "were different enough from theirs to place a space between us." Dickens is too much "the young gentleman"[20] to produce a consistent critique yet. The audience he reprimands he also desires; he derides its "delicacy" but shares and aspires to its system of values. He seeks all the money, status, and emotional sustenance he can from it.[21] "I know," Dickens wrote Forster, "that I have lounged about the streets, insufficiently and unsatisfactorily fed. I know that, but for the mercy of God, I might easily have been, for any care that was taken of me, a little robber or a little vagabond."[22] *Oliver Twist*, the first novel to dramatize Dickens' complex structure of feeling, is written from a hysterical sense of threat; it is as though, in 1838, Dickens can hardly believe that he is not, after all, "a little robber or a little vagabond." The exaggerated, the heightened, quality of the novel's presentations — its Manichaean tension of which Graham Greene speaks[23] — relates directly to this crippling sense of immanent menace. The strategies of the art follow from the complex and raw, the unassimilated, emotions of fear and anger.

III

Arnold Kettle's emphasis on the generalized, symbolic character of Dickens' writing up to chapter 10 of the novel (Brownlow's first appearance) must remain the major critical judgment because Kettle's discrimination illuminates the crucial disjunction in *Oliver Twist*. Yet even within those ten chapters, Oliver's name appears no less than 285 times, an average of 28 to each chapter of an average length of seven pages. This is not counting such reinforcing epithets as "poor boy," "poor little wretch," and so forth, repeatedly used to define Oliver. If these are included, the score mounts to 400 or more. On the face of it, this seems a quantitative trick, except that the arithmetic is proof of Dickens' intense, exclusive concentration upon a *particular* case. The only other suffering child mentioned is Dick, and Dick's entire function in the novel is to die.[24] (In the next chapter we shall see how Dick's case is an important pointer to Dickens' structural strategies in *Nicholas Nickleby*, *The Old Curiosity Shop*, and *Dombey and Son*.) The energy of the hurt in the first section of *Oliver Twist* issues, then, from a sharply personalized anger, illustrated, for example, by the following well-known passage:

I wish some well-fed philosopher, whose meat and drink turn to gall within him; whose blood is ice, whose heart is iron; could have seen Oliver Twist clutching at the dainty viands that the dog had neglected. I wish he could have witnessed the horrible avidity with which Oliver tore the bits asunder with all the ferocity of famine. There is only one thing I should like better; and that would be to see the Philosopher making the same sort of meal himself, with the same relish. (Ch. 4)

There is not even a pretense of distance here. The ferocity of the writing is a naked ferocity; the outrage rises from the heart as unmediated curse. The brutality of the experiential moment is a personally felt brutality. Dickens sees himself as protagonist.

The strength of this unequivocal commitment to Oliver, declared at the outset—"For the next eight or ten months, Oliver was the victim of a systematic course of treachery and deception" (ch. 2)—generates the caustic force of Dickens' satire as well as the untransmuted vocabulary of self-pitying sentiment. The extremity with which Oliver-Dickens feels the presentation determines the perspectives from which the adult world of "wisdom and experience" (ch. 2) is seen and judged. Given Oliver's status as pure victim, with no resource of countering and no combative intelligence—such as the Dodger's toughness of mind or, later, Paul Dombey's questioning ability—the world that surrounds him acquires an appropriately demonic aspect. In a world in which Oliver is counted a mere "item" (ch. 1) there is nobody and nothing he can turn to for protection, for a recognition of his exclusivity. Yet, Dickens is by no means at a point of readiness to allow Oliver to go under. And being more than a protagonist, being also the author, Dickens can provide the succor that the enacted reality cannot, or will not. Dickens will administer "the mercy of God" unto himself.

Our first rather special curiosity about Oliver is evoked as early as chapter 1. Dickens observes: "Wrapped in the blanket which had hitherto formed his only covering, he might have been the child of a nobleman or a beggar; it would have been hard for the haughtiest stranger to have fixed his station in society." The sameness of the parish covering is deplorable because it hides Oliver's "station in society." ("But I held some station at the blacking warehouse too," Dickens had said of himself.)[25] It is of course the earliest hint we have — one that gives away Dickens *a priori* — of Oliver's nobility of birth, which, notwithstanding the talk of "the principle of good" and so forth, we are to understand as having social force ("station"). So that when Dickens goes on with the tickling puzzle in the subsequent chapter — "But nature or inheritance had implanted a good sturdy spirit in Oliver's breast" — we know already the "nature" to be a ploy and the "inheritance" the real thing. That, as it turns out, is to be the squeaky burden of the plot. Dickens has a long way to go indeed to stop seeking shortcuts to "salvation," to acknowledge with the full distance of art that it must lie outside the system-perpetuating personal dream as well as outside the noble, but at bottom, resentful, guilt-generating death. But, for the moment, Oliver must successfully escape the stifling world of coffins and coal cellars, leave the dying Dick behind to "dream so much of Heaven, and Angels, and kind faces," and set out to "seek my fortune" (ch. 7). Only with *David Copperfield* will Dickens begin to dramatize something of what is involved in the seeking of fortune (David speaks of cutting his way through a "forest of difficulty"); and not until *Great Expectations* will fortune have fully changed definition for him. At this early stage of fright and wanting, fortune will simply be given to Oliver. The more ominously he is pressed the more easily it will be given.

And fortune does seem rather heavily stacked in Oliver's favor. One miracle follows another. The "half blind" magistrate who has taken Gamfield for "an honest, open-hearted man" because he is unable to see Gamfield's "villainous countenance" recovers his vision with astonishing alacrity, decipher's Oliver's "pale and terrified face," and prevents himself from signing what could have been Oliver's doom (ch. 3). Oliver's escape from Sowerberrys' establishment turns out a simple affair. In the thieves' den Oliver finds rollicking company and better food than he has had before. His first so-called mishap leads him directly to the patriarch who is to recover all his usurped rights and comforts; his second mishap throws him into the lap of the angelic aunt who will supply him with quantities of cuddling endearment. "Something in that boy's face" "touches and interests" Brownlow, not because the boy is a "vessel of Grace," but because the boy's face recalls to his mind another, a more familiar face—that of the woman whose picture hangs in his living room. Brownlow's wonderment—"Where have I seen something like that look before?" (ch. 11)—has no relation to any providential information. Dickens' fuzzily mystifying and vacuous phraseology ("something in that boy's face") is simply a bad case of detective writing rather than of any profound metaphysical suggestiveness. And in speaking of Oliver as the "principle of Good," Dickens is quite simply thinking of a shivering little boy who will not thieve or be ungrateful if only someone takes charge of him. The only demonstration the novel actually furnishes of Oliver's goodness follows closely along this structure of feeling: it is embodied in Oliver's sense of guilt at what must seem his ingratitude towards his benefactor after he is retaken by Nancy. Also, only in Nancy's struggle does Oliver function as a motive. And ironically, it is in Nancy's struggle rather than in Oliver's that we see anything of the "principle of Good" seeking to recover itself from under the weight of sinfulness, if the novel *were* to be read as a moral parable. Even here, of course, there is difficulty. Nancy's strength is in seeing clearly the reality of the power structure over which Fagin rules,[26] but the all-important clarity of how Fagin's establishment is only a version of Bumble's is kept from her. Nor is she given, as I suggested earlier, the insight which Shaw provides Mrs. Warren: that her guilt is socially imposed through definitions coded by a sanctioned authority structure, the very authority structure that has pushed her and the others into the underworld (Dickens' Preface). Nancy's strength is therefore crucially compromised in the scenes in which Dickens' tactic is to make her feel ashamed, valueless, fallen into a "life of sin," to get her to be her own worst accuser ("I am the infamous creature") and demean her out of her own mouth ("The poorest women fall back, as I make my way along the crowded pavement") when in the presence of Maylie and Brownlow. Nancy's decision to go back to Sikes, perhaps the single most exemplary instance of a triumph of character and commitment portrayed in the novel, is "madness" to Rose Maylie. Nancy is made to speak of her "rotten heart" which cannot shed its attachment to Sikes, "the most desperate among them all" (ch. 40). And in spite of the forceful symbolic use Dickens makes of her death, the suggestion strongly remains that such lives as hers are unredeemable. That is the view the British middle class would take.[27]

Steven Marcus's question "Who is Fagin?"[28] invites a corresponding question: "Who is Borwnlow?" Inside the novel the two together generate the morality-play opposition that has often been noted. Dialectically, however, if Fagin is real — and the whole force of the novel's paranoia derives from that reality — then Brownlow is necessary. The novel makes it clear that the worlds of the bourgeois state and of the thieves' den are not at all antithetical. The principles upon which state institutions run and state officials conduct themselves are the same as those Fagin expounds to Mr. Bolter in chapter 43. Fagin, in fact, is the theoretician and the ideologue for the state as well. Mrs. Mann's "very accurate perception of what was good for herself" (ch. 2) is widely shared — by Bumble, Mrs. Corney, Sowerberry, and Gamfield, who also, after all, performs a social function of some risk; and the gentlemen of the Board translate Fagin's principles to the benefit of a whole class. Community, or banding together, is in both places informed by enlightened self-interest or, in Fagin's eloquent formulation, by regard for the "magic number one." In fact, the underworld, insofar as it is (according to the terms of Dickens' Preface) the creation of the state's application of the "number one" philosophy, knows best the efficacy of that philosophy. Consequently, and ironically, Fagin also knows that the very same philosophy that pushes the thieves into crime best ensures their own survival as a unit: if every thief has regard for his number one, he cannot but hang together with all the rest.[29] Fagin knows too that bourgeois respectability offers a good cover. Thus, whenever Fagin is not alone or plotting with Monks or Sikes, he walks "in imitation of the manner in which old gentlemen walk about the streets" (ch. 9). Charley Bates advises Oliver to put himself "under Fagin" so as to "be able to retire on your property, and do the genteel" (ch. 18). The marvelous Dodger, the picaroon par excellence, knows when to invoke British constitutional practices to shame state officials in charge of implementing those practices: the Dodger, as an "Englishman," asks, "Where are my priwileges?" (ch. 43). Finally, the interchangeable status of these two worlds is established through the transferred destinies of Bumble and Charley Bates. Bumble falls into criminality, and Bates, we are told, "succeeded in the end" and "is now the merriest young grazier in all Northampton-shire." Even Claypole "realizes a genteel subsistence" (ch. 53).

Given this correspondence between these two worlds — both immoral and unjust, the official more so than the other — and given also the terms in which Dickens sees salvation at this point in his career, he has the need to create an arbitrary counter and referent for Oliver's destiny.[30] Brownlow is thus the finished point towards which Oliver must be guided. Brownlow's class, property, prestige, and power together constitute a *fait accompli* into which Oliver must be assimilated. For that reason, Brownlow's reality must simply be assumed, as is Oliver's. Together they are the two ends of one exceptional fate. Dickens' incestuous description clearly suggests this coalescing situation: "Mr. Brownlow adopted Oliver as his son. Removing with him and the old housekeeper to within a mile of the parsonage-house, where his dear friends resided, he gratified the only remaining wish of Oliver's warm and earnest heart and thus linked together a little society, whose condition approached as nearly to one of perfect happiness as can ever be known in this changing world" (ch. 53). If ever there was the fulfillment of the bourgeois dream, this is it. Oliver has *become* Brownlow and, like Fagin's double, has "linked together a little society" as the Edenic opposite. From a chronological reading of the endings of Dickens' novels, one may have a fair sense of the curve of his development. Where the whole novel here has been engineered towards this ending, towards something desperately to be believed in, the ending of *Great Expectations* remains basically a matter of indifference to Dickens because experience there replaces wish fulfillment. The only saving grace about Dickens' description of the closure of the Brownlow paradise is in the unsettling last phrase of the paragraph — "changing world." Even in the most cuddled and snug moment Dickens' genius asserts itself. The "changing world" is what he must go on to enact.

CHAPTER 3

Nicholas Nickleby and The Old Curiosity Shop: The Split Self-Image

I

Mikhail Bakhtin writes of Dostoevsky that he "strives to make two persons out of every contradiction in order to dramatize the contradiction and reveal it extensively."[1] It is a strategy—as the expression of a deep experiential dilemma—that Dickens also uses in the early novels. There is no doubt a difference. In Dostoevsky contradictions are fully sentient, and thus fully exploited in the art. In Dickens the split self-image first emerges as a hidden duality in *Oliver Twist*, but as he moves on, he is able to employ it with enhanced control and critical charge, until a momentous reversal takes place in *David Copperfield* in the status of the thesis and the anti-thesis. Let me proceed to show what I mean.

In chapter 7 of *Oliver Twist* Oliver, running away from Sowerberry's establishment, meets Dick at the workhouse. He tells Dick that he has been "beat and ill-used" and is "going to seek my fortune, some long way off." Dick informs Oliver that he has "heard the doctor tell them I was dying" but urges Oliver not to "stop" on his account. Oliver, indeed, does not stop: "Yes, yes, I will, to say good-bye to you. . . . I shall see you again, Dick. I know I

36

shall! You will be well and happy!" Dick is, understandably, not so sanguine about meeting Oliver again, except "after I am dead." He knows "the doctor must be right because I dream so much of Heaven, and Angels, and kind faces that I never see when I am awake." In the end, Dick says, "God bless you," and Oliver leaves. When the salvaged Oliver returns to the old places with the Brownlow entourage (ch. 51), he remembers Dick and resolves that "we'll take him away from here, and have him clothed and taught, and send him to some quiet country place where he may grow strong and well." Rose Maylie concurs: "You will see him soon. . . . You shall tell him how happy you are, and how rich you have grown, and that in all your happiness you have none so great as the coming back to make him happy too." Unhappily, however, Oliver soon discovers that "Poor Dick was dead!"

Admittedly, in reading *Oliver Twist* one does not think of Dick with any measure of autonomous significance; one thinks of Dick as an unfortunate victim of the system, and one is rushed on to the pressing claims of Oliver's destiny. Yet, strategically, Dick is to be differentiated from the rest of the poorhouse orphans in that we are given, however passingly, a sense of his particular relation to and claims on Oliver. Upon Oliver's return in "triumph," his first thought is for Dick. He wished to do for Dick what Brownlow, Mrs. Bedwin, and Rose have done for him – clothe him, teach him, and make him strong. Dick, sadly, has forestalled all this and died, dreaming, no doubt, of "Heaven, and Angels." The situation of Dick and Oliver presents embryonically the structure of ambivalence which is to become the central organizing principle of experience and art in *Nicholas Nickleby* and *The Old Curiosity Shop*; it informs *Dombey and Son* as well, but at a significant critical remove. Philip Collins and Angus Wilson have commented on the more obvious aspect of this situation, the death of the child in Dickens' early fiction. However, a dialectical analysis of the Dick-Oliver concatenation as it develops in *Nicholas Nickleby* and *The Old Curiosity Shop* (and later in *Dombey and Son*) alters our understanding of Dickens' early work in a way that also affects our sense of the strength, or the ongoing *reality*, of Dickens' introspections.

Collins provides a point of entry into a consideration of what

I see as the dialectic of the split self-image in *Oliver Twist, Nicholas Nickleby,* and *The Old Curiosity Shop*: "Oliver dies by proxy, in the person of his workhouse friend, 'poor little Dick.'"[2] Collins' statement points to the paradox of surrogacy: Oliver dies in Dick. Yet the meat of the matter lies, I suggest, in our recognition that whereas Oliver dies as Dick, he does not die as Oliver: he makes good. Admittedly, his moment of secure happiness is clouded temporarily by news of Dick's death, but his happiness has first been secured, and the cloud (really a mere puff) is too obviously a gesture. Now, this summary suggestion of surrogate images expands into the focal point of structural and cultural interest in the novels under consideration here.

In speaking of *Oliver Twist* I argued that Dickens' sense of personal menace is so total that it obliges him to concentrate the major energies of his art on confounding that menace (in the process, also confounding the power of his intended demonstration) and on ensuring the spectacular fall of his enemies (the Sikes hunt, Fagin and the courtroom full of "eyes"). Consequently, Dick receives limited attention in the action of that novel, serving what seems like a passing function. The peremptory nature of that attention as well as its attendant irony is illustrated best by the expedient haste of Oliver's interview with Dick in chapter 7. Dick — who, along with the early Oliver, in his status as the total victim, is posited as the thesis which informs Dickens' indictment — is, under the pressure of intense personal wishfulness, pushed out and relegated by the later Oliver, the anti-thesis. A further stage in Dickens' self-confrontation is now marked by a resurrection of Dick — as Smike in *Nicholas Nickleby,* as Nell in *The Old Curiosity Shop,* as Paul in *Dombey and Son* — for a more elaborate martyrdom. The action of these novels is more centrally burdened with the pain of dissolution. At the same time, though he seeks to project his self-image by transcending bourgeois Victorian values, such transcendence is, in actuality, illusory and unsatisfactory to Dickens.[3] Hence, whereas, on the one hand, Dickens seeks to cling rather desperately to an unfelt doctrine of future reward, on the other, being plainly unconvinced and still very much enticed by the categories of success sanctioned by the culture, he simultaneously provides more material satisfaction to the surrogate selves of the children who die: for Smike there is Nicholas; for Nell, Kit (and for Paul, Florence and Walter Gay). I shall attempt to delineate the significant contours of development within this common structure in the novels, the ways in which the martyred self becomes an increasingly more sophisticated and distanced critique of the culture.

The contemporary response, popular and critical, to these novels shows that Dickens' schizoid needs and allegiances conform directly to and express the schizophrenia of bourgeois Victorian culture. How else are we to explain the hysterical approval (clearly guilt-generated) accorded the deaths of Smike, Nell, and Paul and, simultaneously, the happy conclusions of the destinies of Nicholas, Kit, Dick Swiveller, and Walter Gay? (The severance between the popular and the critical responses does not occur, really, until the 1880s, with Oscar Wilde, understandably, sounding the first shocking intimation of the arrival of new taste by his very self-conscious, though amusing, reference to Nell.)[4] Self-flagellation and success go hand in hand. *Nicholas Nickleby* and *The Old Curiosity Shop* present the contradiction between the thesis and the anti-thesis, structurally, in its most blatant form. With *Martin Chuzzlewit* Dickens, as he sees the driving impetus of the culture more clearly, begins to mitigate the contradiction: old Martin is rich but not entirely good, and young Martin must exert himself somewhat before he is rewarded. *Dombey and Son* offers the most aware and coherent engagement yet with the contradiction, except for the compromise in the case of Walter Gay, a compromise which Dickens makes consciously and against his better judgment, suggesting, paradoxically, a new critical toughness and consistency of response.

II

Much of what I have to say about the structure of *Nicholas Nickleby* is already implied in Steven Marcus's perceptive essay. No reading which considers *Nicholas Nickleby* by and for itself can, however, hope to resurrect it as, in any sense, a classic for a modern critical audience. But when viewed in the context of the developing synthesis I suggested earlier, *Nicholas Nickleby* finds an intelligible place in the oeuvre—a place more intelligible than the one given it by Bernard Bergonzi's suggestion that "it is as a fairy tale, the embodiment of the childlike vision of the world that *Nicholas Nickleby* must ultimately be read."[5] Ultimately, this reading amounts only to a familiar prescriptive fallacy. Beyond a point, no alterations in mere methodology (or classroom pedagogy) can redeem the substantive thinness of a book or load the poverty of its experience.

Nicholas Nickleby, in the contradictory function of its character clusters, is principally organized around the destinies of Nicholas and Smike, who are, as Marcus tells us, "two sides of a single person."[6] The fact that these two boys, who are of the same age, are held together as "constant companions" (ch. 61) throughout the action of the novel is, of course, the best and the most obvious evidence of their status as surrogates for each other. A closer look, however, reveals the assiduity of detail with which Dickens consolidates this surrogate structure. Brought together early at Dotheboys Hall, Smike's first "painful" look "went to Nicholas's heart at once" (ch. 7). As Squeers' distrust and dislike of Nicholas grow, "all the spleen and ill-humour that could not be vented on Nicholas were unceasingly bestowed" upon "this poor being [Smike]." "It was no sooner observed that he had become attached to Nicholas, than stripes and blows . . . morning, noon, and night, were his only portion"; Smike "paid for both" (ch. 12). Smike makes Nicholas's "heart ache at the prospect of the suffering he was destined to undergo," and Nicholas's one rousing action in the novel is undertaken directly on behalf of Smike: "Touch him at your peril! I will not stand by, and see it done," says Nicholas to Squeers. When Nicholas, having chastised Squeers, decides to leave "this foul den" where "dastardly cruelties [are] practised on helpless infancy," Smike wishes, henceforth, "only . . . to be near you." Nicholas answers: "And you shall . . . And the world shall deal by you as it does by me, till one or both of us shall quit it for a better" (ch. 13). In each of Nicholas's peregrinations Smike becomes a co-traveler. When Nicholas leaves London for Portsmouth, believing himself, rather easily, to be the cause of Ralph's neglect of his mother and sister, he says to Smike, "We will journey from this place together," for "my heart is linked to yours" (ch. 20). At

Master Crummles' theatre company Smike is introduced to Mrs. Vincent Crummles, immediately after Nicholas, as "the other" (ch. 23). Back in London, Smike is to be thought of as "one of our own little household, wherever we live, or whatever fortune is in reserve for us" (ch. 35). Finally, Nicholas and Smike are together as the cycle of the novel's action is completed in their return to the old sites in Yorkshire, where Nicholas, "ever at [Smike's] side," watches, with no one else present, the death of "the partner of his poverty and the sharer of his better fortune" (ch. 58).

This then is an advance over the Dick-Oliver presentation. Whereas Oliver parts from Dick as early as chapter 7 of that novel, Nicholas and Smike are held together inseparably. As dramatic presentations Smike and Nicholas fail indefensibly. Yet, Dickens' willingness to give — as author and through Nicholas — a central attention to Smike is the beginning of the confrontation that will lead, through a protracted process, to the secure and complex art of *Great Expectations*. The death of Smike is informed with a cultural meaning that is of major significance with regard to Dickens' further movement: Smike is Ralph Nickleby's son. The central irony of the book — the irony which defines the dimension of Dickens' exploration in *Nicholas Nickleby* — is sounded when Ralph, is his desperation to destroy Nicholas, is made to wish that he "could strike him through this boy [Smike]" (ch. 34). In wishing to avenge himself against Nicholas, unknowingly through his own blood, Smike, Ralph destroys himself in the very attic which comprises Smike's only memory of his past ("I remember I slept in a room, a large lonesome room at the top of a house, where there was a trap-door in the ceiling" [ch. 22]). Ralph "had torn a rope from one of the old trunks, and hanged himself on an iron hook immediately below the trap-door in the ceiling — in the very place to which the eyes of his son, a lonely, desolate little creature, had so often been directed in childish terror fourteen years before" (ch. 62). Smike's death, then, signifies two things: a painful (to Dickens) rejection of what Ralph calls the "power of money" (ch. 28), since Smike will not inherit his father's wealth; and a recognition that the countering moral power generated by the suffering of the victim can hurt the oppressor, who can be one's own father.

The suffering and death of Smike are to be seen, then, as a response both to parental and institutional failures which Dickens comments on in well-known, though isolated, passages (chs. 4, 8, 32, 50, 53), and to the moral philosophy of the "magic number one," which after *Oliver Twist* finds renewed expression in Squeers' exchange with Ralph when things begin to go bad for both: "Well, if all goes right now, that's quite correct, and I don't mind it; but if anything goes wrong, then, times are altered, and I shall just say and do whatever I think may serve me most . . . the only number in all arithmetic that I know of . . . is number one, under this here most fatal go!" (ch. 60). The authorities of parent, teacher, and society, rolled into the figures of Ralph and Squeers—who are accordingly linked in a common exploitative intrigue against the oppressed—are denied and defeated by the child through his martyrdom, both in the power they exert and in the quality of success they embody. This, however, is not enough for Dickens. The need for vindication remains strong, and the vindication offered is twofold. First, the "slow decline" of the victim into death is sought to be projected as a "reward": "He fell into a light slumber, and waking, smiled as before; then spoke of beautiful gardens, which he said stretched out before him, and were filled with figures of men, women, and many children, all with light upon their faces; then whispered that it was Eden—and so died" (ch. 58). Contrarily, knowing that this reward is a rationalization, unfelt because unsought (by Smike and Dickens alike), Dickens keeps in motion the machinery of the plot in order to obtain for the surrogate of the resentfully and reluctantly martyred child such material recognitions as the martyrdom is, in the first place, meant to repudiate. Thus, we are given Nicholas, Madeline Bray (for the Kate Smike could not possess), and the Cheeryble Brothers (as antitheses to Ralph, Squeers, and Gride).

In relation to Dickens' central problem, Nicholas's employment at Dotheboys Hall raises for him, and for Dickens, a rather fundamental question: can he, should he, find for himself a place within a prevailing "system" that he has seen to be corrupt and unjust? Depressed by what he has witnessed of Squeers' establishment, Nicholas feels "self-degraded by the consciousness of his position"; "he actually seemed . . . to be the aider and abettor of a system which filled him with honest disgust and indignation." Guilt-ridden and ashamed, "he loathed himself, and felt, for the moment, as though the mere consciousness of his present situation must, through all time to come, prevent his raising his head again." This is a question, however, that must wait for its full exploration until Pip's situation with Magwitch. As for Nicholas, "his resolve was taken, and the resolution he had formed on the preceding night [the resolution to let things be] remained undisturbed" (ch. 8). For what appears an interminable interval of time, Nicholas "broods," or merely grinds his teeth "at every repetition of the savage and cowardly attack" (ch. 12), or, as befits a "young gentle-man" (ch. 22) with "an aristocratic air" (ch. 15), "content[s] himself with darting a contemptuous look at the tyrant, and walk[s], as majestically as he could, up stairs" (ch. 14).[7] Nicholas, "speaking more to my own thoughts than to [Smike]," knows now that he "shall be driven to [leaving his employment] at last," for "the world is before me, after all" (ch. 12). Smike's world, such as it is, has been conditioned by the powers that presided at his birth — Ralph, Brooker, Squeers; therefore, Nicholas's world shall be "before me," a world and destiny calculated to vindicate Smike, his alter ego.

Nicholas and Ralph meet in chapter 3. Immediately, Dickens asserts a moral opposition between the two upon the ground that whereas Ralph's visage shows "avarice and cunning," Nicholas's face is "bright with the light of intelligence and spirit." Thus, "there was an emanation from the warm young heart in his look and bearing which kept the old man down." The only objective correlative of the "emanation" will be Nicholas's favored status with Noggs, La Creevy, and Linkinwater, just as Mrs. Bedwin's and Nancy's serendipitous conviction about Oliver was the proof offered of Oliver's goodness. When Ralph is told of the discomfiture of Lord Frederick and Mulberry Hawk at the hands of Nicholas, he "beat his foot impatiently upon the ground" and concluded that "there is some spell about that boy. . . . Circumstances conspire to help him. Talk of fortune's favours! What is even money to such devil's luck as this!" (ch. 44). The "spell," the "fortune," the "luck," are all reminiscent of the contrived mythology that attached to Oliver. "Circumstances" are indeed to be manipulated to ensure the successes of Nicholas, and the successes will be in sterling. The sterling of bad men like Ralph can, however, hardly be clean enough for Nicholas: "But they [Ralph's heirs] could not bear the thought of growing rich on money so acquired, and felt as though they could never hope to prosper with it. They made no claim to his wealth" (ch. 65). Hence the need for good men with great stores of clean sterling.

On the occasion of Nicholas's first encounter with those "good-natured and astonishingly clean-handed tycoons,"[8] the Brothers Cheeryble, the brothers permit themselves the indulgence of reminiscing about "the time when we were two friendless lads, and earned our first shilling in this great city" (ch. 35). The reader is left to assume that thereafter the propitious "first shilling," through the alchemy performed upon it by the sheer goodness of the Brothers Cheeryble, multiplied itself *ad infinitum* without obliging its possessors to soil either their own integrity or the integrity of others in the process. Indeed, it is the process, precisely, that is missing. Nor may we ask how it is that the unstoppable charity of the Cheerybles does not threaten the liquidation of their empire.[9] Critics (like Bergonzi) will tell us that the Cheeryble brothers are really not human constructs but fairy godfathers. Dickens, on the other hand, insists that he had living models for these "gruesome old Peter Pans"[10] in the Grant brothers of Manchester. The point about the Cheerybles is that Dickens, given his continuing need, must still believe in the possibility of the Cheerybles, even while he sees how money leads to greed, and greed to Gride. He is therefore more than willing, at this stage of his development, to substitute, without question, the *reputation* of the Cheerybles for their *reality*. Thus, "their function seems to be to exorcise (most unconvincingly) the terrors of the crude and virile industrialism of the 1830s. They represent business without balance sheets, without labour troubles, without competitions, without anxiety."[11] So long as Dickens has a goal for himself within that culture, the structures of his fiction must project that goal — the man who is at once rich and good. Therefore his assumption will be that it is man who vitiates money, rather than money that vitiates man. This assumption informs not only the Cheerybles but Ralph Nickleby as well. We are told of Ralph that he "was not, strictly speaking, what you would call a merchant, neither was he a banker, nor an attorney, nor a special pleader, nor a notary. He was certainly not a tradesman, and still less could he lay any claim to the title of a professional gentleman; for it would have been impossible to mention any recognized profession to which he belonged" (ch. 2). This denies Ralph any particular social identity. His money is bad because he is bad; it is therefore of no account how his money was made (usury would hardly seem the most ingenious investment technique). Correspondingly, the Cheeryble money is good because the Cheerybles are good; again, it is of no account how their money was made. Dickens' willful naïveté is a direct expression of his pressing ambivalence. Mrs. Nickleby's pretensions, her hopes for her son, her dreams of Kate's ascension into the aristocracy through the attentions of some titled game hunter (at the Mantalinis or the Wititterlys), may be laughable; what is not laughable, however, is Nicholas's answer to Smike's "shall I ever see your sister?": "To be sure," says Nicholas, "we shall be all together one of these days—when we are rich, Smike" (ch. 29). Unlike the expectations of Richard Carstone, Pip, or Charley Hexam, Nicholas's will indeed be fulfilled, Dickens being the arbiter. Nicholas will work hard, impress Linkinwater as Linkinwater has never been impressed, and find a place for himself. Soon Madeline's wretched old father, by dying at just the most helpful moment, will prove how the schemes of the wicked are "overthrown by Heaven" (ch. 54). Nicholas will correctly advise his mother and Kate not to harbor designs on Frank Cheeryble, because "remember how poor we are" (ch. 55). (One has only to think of Eugene Wrayburn and Lizzie Hexam or John Harmon and Bella Wilfer to see the distance Dickens will travel.) All the while, of course, Nicholas will be thinking that sooner rather than later "I may grow rich" (ch. 61). And, indeed, Madeline's "fortune being destined to be yours" (ch. 63), according to the dispensation of the Brothers Cheeryble, Nicholas will come into a truly impressive chunk of sterling, £12,000 to be exact. This he will promptly invest, or feed back, into Cheeryble enterprises (whatever they be) and soon after become a Cheeryble himself. Happiness will remain related to money ("if Nicholas had had ten thousand pounds, he would . . . have bestowed its utmost farthing . . . to secure [Madeline's] happiness" [ch. 61]), being, ultimately, lost or secured by it. The worlds of the Kenwigses and the Mantalinis, even the Crummleses, remain on the outside,[12] to provide the fun, while, thanks to what Nicholas thinks of as the "excellence and munificence of the brothers Cheeryble" (ch. 37), he plucks goodly "plums from Fortune's choicest pudding" (ch. 35) as the Cheerybles, those two "friendless lads" of old, have successfully plucked before. Thus Dickens' faith in himself and in his culture is restored, even while Smike's destiny threatens to dissolve it.

III

The more considerable discussions of *The Old Curiosity Shop*, although opposed in their approaches to its experience, seem, curiously, to converge on one significant point. The book, we are told, is not a novel about "society." Steven Marcus, writing on Nell's behalf, contends that "in *The Old Curiosity Shop* society does not exist in any significant sense, the concentrated duality of Nell and Quilp has almost obliterated that middle ground"—the "middle ground" that is represented by the Nubbleses, the Brasses, Dick Swiveller, the marchioness, Barbara, and the school master.[13] (Of the laborers and the workers out of work I shall speak later.) Gabriel Pearson, writing "Quilpiad," holds that "the asocial, fairy-tale setting of Quilp and Nell effectively disables any social actuality."[14] Of the two, Pearson's comment, insofar as it is an aesthetic summation, seems to me intelligible. I do not know what Marcus means, though, when he finds "society" missing in *The Old Curiosity Shop*.

It is certainly clear (as some of the more tentative accounts of the novel suggest) that Victorian society of the late 1830s and the early 1840s is most markedly, and disturbingly, present in *The Old Curiosity Shop*. There is, however, a significant change in Dickens' mode of perception of this society, and this is the reason, perhaps, that critics find "society" absent from the novel: there are no "issues" in *The Old Curiosity Shop*. It is, I think, the first novel in which Dickens begins to perceive his society as a general condition. Correspondingly, Dickens' thesis, embodied in Nell, now projects a qualitatively different response to the differently perceived reality—a response as general and as philosophical as Dickens' perception of his society begins to be. Yet, along with this, the pain involved in the effort of renunciation suggests Dickens' continued vulnerability and makes intelligible the treatment of Nell's surrogate, Kit Nubbles. Dickens' ambivalence is once again apparent in the structure of the novel.

The morning that Nell and her grandfather leave London (ch. 15), he "press[es] his finger on his lip" and draws the child along "by narrow courts and winding ways"; nor does he seem "at ease until they had left it far behind, often casting a backward look towards it, murmuring that ruin and self-murder were crouching in every street, and would follow if they scented them." Clearly, London is presented as a city full of menace: "ruin and self-murder" crouch in "every street." Thereupon follows further detail, social detail, reminiscent of *Oliver Twist*, detail of "rags and paper" that make up "the populous poverty that sheltered there." The "shops sold goods that only poverty could buy, and sellers and buyers were pinched and griped alike. Here were poor streets where faded gentility essayed with scanty space and ship-wrecked means to make its last feeble stand, but tax-gatherer and creditor came there as elsewhere, and the poverty that yet faintly struggled was hardly less squalid and manifest than that which had long ago submitted and given up the game." There is both a visual and a tonal quality about Dickens' focus on the "rags and paper" and on the street which suggests the Eliot of "Preludes" and "Prufrock." Even the tax-gatherer and the creditor are not so dated after all, only computerized. At the time that Dickens was writing, however, the assault of the "tax-gatherer and creditor," the visible tentacles of a new, exploitive social and financial order, left the fading gentility and the proletariat alike with very little to live by, or live for. Dickens' detailing is comprehensive: "Damp, rotten houses," "children, scantily fed and clothed . . . sprawling in the dust," "scolding mothers," "shabby fathers," "mangling-women, washer-women, cobblers, tailors, chandlers, driving their trades in parlours and kitchens and back rooms and garrets . . . all of them under the same roof," "houses burnt down and blackened and blistered by the flames," "rank confusion" yielding an "illustration" of "the miseries of Earth" (ch. 15).

As we follow the "two pilgrims" to Mrs. Jarley's waxworks, to the grandfather's meeting with the gypsies and his temptation to steal (in which he is thwarted by Nell), we reach the high point of their suffering; we reach, at the novel's center, the Industrial Midlands of the Black Country. There, Nell is accosted by a "black figure" which comes "suddenly out of the dark recess" in which they are "about to take refuge." This "form" is "of a man, miserably clad and begrimed with smoke" who, nonetheless, offers the "two pilgrims" a "bed of warm ashes." In the "dark sky" can be seen "hanging" a "lurid glare," the "dull reflection of some distant fire." As this "form" carries Nell gently "inside" (under the circumstances, a tribute to the humanity of the proletariat), this is what we see:

In a large and lofty building, supported by pillars of iron, with great black apertures in the upper walls, open to the external air; echoing to the roof with the beating of hammers and roar of furnaces, mingled with the hissing of red-hot metal plunged in water, and a hundred strange unearthly noises never heard elsewhere; in this gloomy place, moving like demons among the flame and smoke, dimly and fitfully seen, flushed and tormented by the burning fires, and wielding great weapons, a faulty blow from any one of which must have crushed some workman's skull, a number of men laboured like giants. Others, reposing upon heaps of coals or ashes with their faces turned to the black vault above, slept or rested from their toil. Others again, opening the white-hot furnace-doors, cast fuel on the flames, which came rushing and roaring forth to meet it, and licked it up like oil. Others drew forth, with clashing noise upon the ground, great sheets of glowing steel, emitting an insupportable heat, and a dull deep light like that which reddens in the eyes of savage beasts. (Ch. 44)

At the heart of the novel's experience, we are given with a searing vividness a vision of the hell that laissez-faire industrialism has turned England into. There is an unmistakable new texture to Dickens' perception. The images of "pillars," "giants," of "savage beasts," of flames licking up the fuel as the "furnace-doors" open, of workers "moving like demons among the flame and the smoke, dimly and fitfully seen, flushed and tormented by the burning fires, and wielding great weapons" which could have easily "crushed some workman's skull" suggest a quality of surrealist penetration into the sickness of Industrial England such as Lawrence will give us.

The very soul of England is, as it were, red with the blood of the damned, laboring demons, with the anguish of mothers whose children are transported for small thefts of food. One such mother, whose transgressing child does not have the extenuation of being either deaf or dumb, unlike the child of another woman, cries: "He was deaf, dumb, and blind, to all that was good and right, from his cradle. Her boy may have learnt no better! where did mine learn better? where could he? who was there to teach him better, or where was it to be learnt?" (ch. 45). These are questions that derive again from Dickens' position in the Preface to *Oliver Twist*. *The Old Curiosity Shop*, we are told meanwhile, is a novel in which "society does not exist in any significant sense." I do not wish to suggest here that Dickens means to take an anti-industrial position, or that he seeks to present an absolute country-town opposition, as has been thought by quite a few readers, who interpret *The Old Curiosity Shop* as Dickens' advocacy of the pastoral. As we know, Dickens disparaged Luddite activity as constituting "the destruction of machinery which was destined to supply unborn millions with employment."[15] The case of Mr. Toodle immediately comes to mind. Dickens' imagery suggests powerfully, however, the wretchedness, the soul-sickness, the alienated world of the Midland factories. What Dickens perceives in *The Old Curiosity Shop* in quasi-demonic or religious metaphor, or in a mode of romantic excess, he presents later on (*Dombey and Son*, *Hard Times*) in rational, systemic terms. The evidence that Dickens is not merely carried away by what he sees as image but is alive to the particular social and philosophical assumptions which inform the seen reality is already, nevertheless, present in *The Old Curiosity Shop*. Miss Monflathers, who reprimands Miss Edwards for having "an attachment to the lower classes" which "all I say and do will not wean you from," has this to say to Nell: "Don't you feel how naughty it is of you . . . to be a wax-work child, when you might have the proud consciousness of assisting, to the extent of your infant powers, the manufacturers of your country; of improving your mind by the constant contemplation of the steam-engine; and of earning a comfortable and independent subsistence of from two-and-ninepence to three shillings per week?" (ch. 31).

Although in the total bulk of the novel "industrial society" remains "localized," being "something you come to, and then rapidly pass through and escape,"[16] it is already discernible how Dickens will move, through *Dombey and Son*, to the concentrated indictment of *Hard Times*.[17] Monflathers' advice to Nell suggests that the concepts and the human negations that underlie capitalist industrialism are beginning to find a clearer resonance with Dickens; its language demonstrates the hard, controlled, and self-assured irony that is to become the mode in the later Dickens.

Dickens, however, has not yet the strength of detachment to enable him to sustain the promise he shows here with Monflathers, to confront and dramatize the fullest implications of the Monflathers (Macaulay?) assumptions. Thus, Dickens' response in *The Old Curiosity Shop* is divided between a spatial and allegedly philosophical escape on the one hand (Nell) and continued self-protection on the other (Kit). It is a response that does not make for a great novel, but one that, in relation to Dickens' self-divided struggle, is both internally consistent and intelligible.

Issuing from this new and more generalized perception of what it is that ails England, Dickens posits the more generalized, but surer, instinct of the child-martyr: "Let us be beggars, and be happy" (ch. 9), Nell says to her grandfather. However sentimentally (however falsely) Dickens treats this perception in the book, it denotes a departure from Oliver and Nicholas, as well as from Dick and Smike in their function as victims who do not formulate an opinion or take a position. Nell's instinct is morally sure and evolved: Nell does not say "Let us be beggars *but* be happy"; she says "Let us be beggars *and* be happy." Nell is not saying happiness may well be found without wealth; she is saying, in fact, that the pursuit of wealth is the pursuit of unhappiness. This is the new affirmation that the experience of Trent and Nell is meant to convey.

Nell is to be seen, therefore, as the victim, not of Quilp, but of her grandfather. Quilp's lust for her is altogether a minor motif compared to his designs on the money he believes the grandfather possesses; after all, he is quite willing to try to have Dick marry her to that larger purpose. The power that Quilp holds over Nell's grandfather derives directly from the old man's speculative ambitions. Such ambitions (that those ambitions are for Nell is only an ironic extenuation) fall into a historical context of what Dyson calls "stock-jobbing and fraudulent financial empires in the city of London." Dyson—who, like Marcus and Pearson, thinks that the novel makes the "social point" only "glancingly" (despite the fact that "some of the greatest writing in the book is to be found in chapters 43 to 45," the Black-Country sections)—rightly points out that Nell's grandfather's "vice" is "little underlined" in terms of its far-reaching connections to those "empires." Dyson's observation underscores the lack, as yet, of rigor in Dickens' relation to his culture and in his art.[18] Nevertheless, Dickens offers in the old man a significantly new situation, a situation that will be more fully developed and exploited in *Dombey and Son.* We have in Nell's grandfather the case of a well-intentioned father figure whose best motives toward his child are vitiated by his speculative pursuit of those motives. This is a step ahead of Ralph Nickleby. Ralph's money was to be rejected because it was tainted by his ill-nature; the old man, on the other hand, is a doting grandfather who goes bad by chasing money and who alienates the object of his affection by the means through which he hopes to secure Nell's happiness. When Quilp discovers where his money has been going, he exclaims, rather sympathetically, "That I should have been blinded . . . by a mere shallow gambler!" The old man's outraged defense is:

I am no gambler. . . . I call Heaven to witness that I never played for gain of mine, or love of play; that at every piece I staked, I whispered to myself that orphan's name and called on Heaven to bless the venture, which it never did. Whom did it prosper? Who were those with whom I played? Men who lived by plunder, profligacy, and riot, squandering their gold in doing ill and propagating vice and evil. My winnings would have been from them . . . bestowed to the last farthing on a young sinless child whose life they would have sweetened and made happy. . . . Who would not have hoped in such a cause? (Ch. 9)

This delusion is the seed-ground from which the ironies of the Magwitch-Pip drama will spring. Already, this defense, although undramatized in the action of the novel, will not do. Can love and the pursuit of wealth be compatible? Can money articulate or ensure humanity? These are the questions that inform the dynamics of Dickens' further movement.

The grandfather's response to Nell's plea is "Beggars—and happy!" Nell's conviction, in turn, is "I have no fear but we shall have enough, I am sure we shall." For Nell the crucial thing is that "If you are sorrowful, let me know why and be sorrowful too; if you waste away . . . let me be your nurse and try to comfort you. If you are poor, let us be poor together" (ch. 9). One is, of course, immediately reminded of Lear and Cordelia, a parallel that Dickens invokes consciously and that has often been noted. In the context of my argument about the nature of the movement in Dickens' perception of himself as victim, what the Cordelia-Lear situation implies is that the victim now exercises a conscious option against self-pitying paralysis (Dick, Oliver, Smike) and for responsibility to another human being. Nell wishes to be identified, not as helpless victim, but as giving adult. The novel flounders precisely because Dickens is not strong enough to allow this.[19] Nell and her grandfather project for the first time the pattern which will be repeated, with greater strength of conviction and art, in Agnes Wickfield, Amy Dorrit, Lizzy Hexam, Jenny Wren, and their correspondingly diminished and dependent father figures. In *The Old Curiosity Shop* Dickens will have us cry, Nell's fortitude notwithstanding. By the time that Dickens' thesis develops to Paul Dombey, Dickens knows what dramatic and moral use he can put that thesis to and how it can be made to subserve a more detached and integrated vision, although even with Paul some of the protective mechanics remain operative.

London, Nell tells her grandfather, is a "sad place." No Brownlow is immediately available; nor is Kit to Nell (as surrogate) quite the same now as Nicholas to Smike, in terms, that is, of his power to succor her. Kit does, indeed, offer shelter to Nell, but Quilp's treachery effectively forestalls her grandfather's acceptance of Kit's offer. This removal of effective protection for the victim inside the novel is, in itself, an expression of Dickens' growing strength. At the same time Nell cannot be allowed to be soiled. Nell and her grandfather are therefore taken out of London on a seemingly never-ending pastoral.

The romantic and mythic dimensions of this pastoral, suggested first by Hillis Miller, are excellently examined by Steven Marcus.[20] As the pastoral lingers, the parallels to the more effete and weakly polemical Wordsworth (the Wordsworth of "We Are Seven"; see ch. 53) multiply, and the diseased burden of its emotion, or what is meant to approximate emotion, gets increasingly centered in death. Marcus shows how Mrs. Jarley's waxworks contribute, classically, to a sense of cold and rotting lifelesseness. Cemeteries proliferate at a frightful rate. As the journey (to no place) comes to an end with the schoolmaster's offer of his house to the "pilgrims," Dickens shifts the experience of Nell into the spiritual gear: "A change had been gradually stealing over her, in the time of her loneliness and sorrow. With failing strength and heightening resolution, there had sprung up a purified and altered mind; there had grown in her bosom blessed thoughts and hopes" (ch. 52). At this point we are back with Richardson in the sanctified though embarrassing world of *Clarissa*. The parallel, I think, illuminates Dickens' problem and strategy quite well. Richardson's initial assumption was that his novel was going to be of the "Tragic Kind."[21] To this end he argued with his irate correspondents (especially Lady Bradshaigh) that his heroine was not meant to be seen as flawless but as implicated in her fate.[22] This did not convince, and pleas for saving Clarissa from her destined end came pouring in, Lady Bradshaigh even threatening that if Richardson did not change his mind she would refuse to read another page.[23] Shifting ground, Richardson argued that Clarissa's death was not, after all, tragic; indeed, it was to be construed as the ultimate "reward."[24] Rather than pity Clarissa as she lovingly courts death, the reader might feel edified and hope for a similar consummation. The problem that arose was, of course, that if this was the case, then *Clarissa* was not the tragedy that Richardson set out to write.

Dickens' ambivalence with respect to Nell is very similar, although aesthetically less complicated. He seeks to charge the protracted sufferings of Nell—an apotheosis of Dick, the early Oliver, and Smike—with a force for active sympathy (such as they generated in the popular readership, as well as in people like Jeffrey, Thackeray, and Carlyle); however, Nell, like Clarrisa, being virtue incarnate, must be rewarded, reward being still much on Dickens' mind, even if not on Nell's. Since by her example Nell repudiates the values of the culture, her reward can come only from Heaven: "She was dead. No sleep so beautiful and calm, so free from trace of pain, so fair to look upon. She seemed a creature fresh from the hand of God, and waiting for the breath of life; not one who had lived and suffered death." The assent of the audience to this is sought and projected through the schoolmaster's rhetorical comment: "It is not on earth that Heaven's justice ends. Think what it is compared with the World to which her young spirit has winged its early flight, and say, if one deliberate wish expressed in solemn terms above this bed could call her back to life, which of us would utter it!" (ch. 71). Dickens is here truly on the edge; he would, from all accounts, have been the first to have that word uttered. This is what he wrote to Forster: "Nobody will miss her like I shall. It is such a very painful thing to me, that I cannot really express my sorrow. Old wounds [referring to Mary Hogarth] bleed afresh when I only think of the way of doing it [killing off Nell]." And most ironically for our argument: "I can't preach to myself the school master's consolation, though I try."[25] Of course Dickens cannot, knowing better than to conflate death with sleep: "We call this a state of childishness, but it is the same poor hollow mockery of it, that death is of sleep. . . . Where, in the sharp lineaments of rigid and unsightly death, is the calm beauty of slumber, telling of rest for the waking hours that are past, and the gentle hopes and loves for those which are to come? Lay death and sleep down, side by side, and say who shall find the two akin" (ch. 12).

When master Humphrey first introduced Kit he entertained a "grateful feeling towards the boy from that minute, for I felt that he was the comedy of [Nell's] life" (ch. 1). Kit is to be the "comedy" of Nell's life, not only in the sense that "she always laughs at . . . Kit" (ch. 1), but also in his larger function as the surrogate cause of the destruction of Nell's pursuers and ill-wishers as well as the surrogate recipient of favors denied to her.

Through the first London section of the novel Nell and Kit are seen together. Kit is not just a service boy at her grandfather's: he is Nelly's champion. Kit's combat with Quilp's boy is precipitated by the latter's description of "Nelly" as "ugly" and by Kit's boast that "my master was obliged to do whatever his master

[Quilp] liked" (ch. 6). Kit's mother (one of the few mothers Dickens endorses) tells us how "every night, when [Nell] — poor thing — is sitting alone at that window, you [Kit] are watching in the open street for fear any harm should come to her, and . . . you never leave the place or come home to your bed though you're ever so tired, till such time as you think she's safe in hers" (ch. 10). After Kit has been falsely accused by Quilp of having told him about her grandfather's "secret way of life," Nell, heartbroken, cries, "Oh, Kit, what *have* you done? You . . . who were almost the only friend I had!" It "grieves" Nell "to part with him . . . but there is no help." As for Kit, he, "insensible to all the din and tumult, remained in a state of utter stupefaction" (ch. 10).

Kit's status as something of a surrogate to Nell is reinforced through Quilp's particular and inexplicable distrust and hatred of him, continuing the pattern from the Bumble-Oliver, Fagin-Oliver, Ralph-Nicholas configurations. Kit, "who bears the main burden of virtue in this novel,"[26] excluding only Nell, becomes the focus for the villainy of Quilp and the Brasses. This is first suggested when Quilp, after Kit's fight with Quilp's boy, warns Kit to be "very careful of yourself" (ch. 6). Soon thereafter, Quilp names Kit as his informant with respect to the grandfather's gambling. This leads to the irrevocability of Kit's parting with Nell, and to her and her grandfather leaving London. Despite the intermittent, sinister but ineffective encounters that the "pilgrims" have with the shadowy Quilp while they are on the road, one clearly has the sense that Nell is effectively out of Quilp's reach. Now, however, Quilp's frustrated but unyielding energy shifts to Kit for a target, Quilp never ceasing to associate Kit with Nell. In chapter 48 Quilp, discovering that the Single Gentleman has been in touch with Kit, determines that "I shall have to dispose of him." Quilp's resolution precipitates into the plot against Kit, hatched and carried out through the combined endeavors of Sally and Samson Brass and, inadvertently, of Dick Swiveller. Quilp, in a frenzy of triumphant "ecstasy" at discovering "Kit a thief" (ch. 60), has an effigy of Kit — "the exact model . . . of the dog"— made; then Quilp "batter[s] the great image until the perspiration stream[s] down his face with the violence of the exercise" (ch. 62).

This is the event which gathers into itself the central moral polarities of the book. Kit—who has of course proved himself worthy of trust simply by being in the place he promised he would be for the Garland Chaise a week after his first fortuitous encounter with the Garlands—is certain that his "innocence will come out" (ch. 63). The subsequent confabulations between Dick and the Garlands on the side of Kit, and the confrontations between the Garlands and the Brasses (all of this reminiscent of the Brownlow-Monks and Cheeryble-Ralph polarization), constitute an element of Dickens' strategies that continues to be arbitrary. Kit's rehabilitation is a foregone conclusion, true, once again, to the pattern of *Oliver Twist* and *Nicholas Nickleby*. The forces that generate the suffering of Nell also involve Kit in a realized plot of villainy. Where Nell is reserved for martyrdom, however, her surrogate will vindicate her by functioning as the agent through whom those forces will be crushed. The pattern of punishment (by proxy) that Julian Moynahan finds (and demonstrates brilliantly) in *Great Expectations* is already present in these less dramatized, less creative situations of surrogacy.[27] The plot against Kit precipitates with a rush the dissolution of Quilp and the Brasses.

The vindication of the self-image through punishment of the villains is still not quite enough, however. The presence of the Garlands suggests Dickens' continued need for the Brownlow figure—his residual need, that is, for belief in his own success and in that of his culture. Thus, Dickens writes to Forster, "The way is clear for Kit now."[28] Dying with Nell, Dickens simultaneously survives with Kit, although the scale of success in relation to Oliver and Nicholas is much reduced.[29] Kit is provided a "grand" reception by the congregation of the virtuous (a foretaste of the grand receptions Dickens is to receive from his reading audiences?), he is presented with a "massive silver watch," "a good post" is "secured for him," and "Kit is the happiest of the happy." "Thus . . . his great misfortune turned out to be the source of all his subsequent prosperity" (chs. 68, 73). Oliver, in the hour of his achieved triumph, returns to Dick, who is dead; *Nicholas Nickleby* ends with the pilgrimage to Smike's grave; *The Old Curiosity Shop* concludes with the adult Kit recounting the story of Nell to his children and taking them out to "the street where she had lived" (ch. 73).

Nell advances Dickens in three ways: by her initial and instinctive distrust of wealth and the pursuit of wealth; by opting for discomfort without any terror of poverty ("She had no thought of hunger or cold, or thirst, or suffering," Dickens says in chapter 12); and by her elevated status from the totally passive and parasitic victim to, morally, an adult, caring for rather than being cared for. On the other hand, Dickens' self-pity overflows and mars the promise and the achievement. Reward remains to him a necessary condition of recognition and self-worth, and unconvinced by his own machinery of angels and an afterlife, he retains a surrogate figure who causes the destruction of the victimizers and upon whom are bestowed the earthly fruits denied to the victim. Nell's granduncle, who has earned "wealth for both brothers," is too late to provide Nell the fortune which her grandfather has been seeking all along and which has remained an illusion: "She is poor now but . . . the time is coming when she shall be rich. It has been a long time coming, but it must come at last; a very long time, but it surely must come. . . . When *will* it come to me!" (ch. 1). In a related sense, Dick Swiveller marks a departure for Dickens. Dick, "who means to marry for money . . . marries the penniless . . . little servant girl," in contrast to Nicholas, who "with the purest of intentions, makes his fortune by marriage."[30] Also, Dick seems to be an advance on Kit. In many ways the repository of extravagances dear to Dickens himself, Dick is yet distanced and dramatized and made a credible force for humanity. Above all, his expectations are cut down to a mere £150 annuity!

More generally, *The Old Curiosity Shop* is important in that its protracted sentimentality ensures a necessary exhaustion in Dickens; one has the sense that Dickens is spent in terms of his unmediated urgency on behalf of himself.[31] The catharsis releases him for a more distanced, more realized self-evaluation, although the process continues to be gradual.

CHAPTER 4

Martin Chuzzlewit: A Note

In Dickens' movement towards a more integrated view of the total ethos of his culture — as distinct from polemics about specific
issues — *Martin Chuzzlewit* takes us more directly towards *Dombey and Son*. As Daleski says, "Fortune hunting . . . is at the centre of all the main ramifications of the plot."[1] The actions of all
the dramatized major characters, as well as their interactions, are
shown to be motivated by the greed for money. The consequences
of pursuing money, to the exclusion of the claims of kinship, even
between father and son, are shown to be heinous. Dickens now
establishes a clear-eyed causal relationship not only between
money and general moral decay but between the pursuit of wealth
and crime: "Oh, Chuff . . . oh, dear old Chuff!" says Anthony
Chuzzlewit, "a voice came into my room to-night, and told me
that this crime began with me. It began when I taught [Jonas] to
be too covetous of what I have to leave, and made the expectation
of it his great business!" (ch. 51). Similarly, Pecksniff, with a fine,
framing irony (of which only he himself is smugly possessed) says
to John Westlock that "money . . . is the root of all evil" (ch. 2).

Even rich old Martin, a figure mediating between Brownlow and Dombey, acknowledges to Pecksniff:

I have gone a rich man, among people of all grades and kinds; relatives, friends, and strangers; among people in whom, when I was poor, I had confidence, and justly, for they never once deceived me then, or, to me, wronged each other. But I have never found one nature, no, not one, in which, being wealthy and alone, I was not forced to detect the latent corruption that lay hid within it, waiting for such as I to bring it forth. . . . I have . . . corrupted and changed the nature of all those who have ever attended on me, by breeding avaricious plots and hopes within them. (Ch. 3)

Old Martin, we notice, establishes here a parallel between Anthony and himself. Clearly, Brownlow begins to look murky. Yet the passage carries within it a continuing philosophical dualism with respect to the question of what is "latent" and what is "induced," a dualism that I have argued is dictated by the urgencies of Dickens' self-division with respect to the contradiction between, on the one hand, his perception and judgment of the commercialism of bourgeois Victorian culture and, on the other, his subjective requirements of it. The irony is centered in our awareness of the discordance between the fact of old Martin's acknowledgment of having "corrupted and changed the nature of all those who ever attended on me" and the fact that his riches will yet be passed on to young Martin, ostensibly without any moral damage, even in the face of his own assertion that he has "never found one nature, no, not one" that survived contact with him. It is a passage, therefore, that helps to localize for us the limits of Dickens' advance; to the extent that Dickens remains unaware of or unable to allow for the irony we perceive, *Martin Chuzzlewit* falls short of *Dombey and Son*. Daleski in his excellent essay notes that "young Martin, though . . . he refers to his relations with his grandfather as having been 'a fair exchange, a barter, and no more' (Ch. 14) is not otherwise indicted by the commercial imagery"; Daleski concludes from this, sympathetically, that the fact "emphasizes that [young Martin's] attempt to make his fortune is different in kind from that of Pecksniff, Jonas, and Tigg."[2] In a novel which (as Daleski shows brilliantly) so centrally expounds the connection between commerce and corruption, to say merely that young Martin's pursuit of fortune is "different in kind" is really only to perpetuate the metaphysical apology.[3] Young Martin is still a self-projection, not just on account of the American trip but more centrally and substantively in line with my main argument. And so long as that is the case, old Martin cannot but remain unaltered in his status as the point of arrival.

Dickens' increasingly creative uneasiness, in accordance with his more forceful perception and dramatization of the ills of his culture, finds its expression in *Martin Chuzzlewit* both in old Martin's uneasiness and in the discomforts young Martin is made to undergo in Eden before he is accepted and rewarded. The nature of old Martin's uneasiness is suggested when he says to young Martin: "There is a kind of selfishness. . . . I have learned it in my own experience of my own breast: which is constantly upon the watch for selfishness in others; and holding others at a distance by suspicions and distrusts, wonders why they don't approach, and don't confide, and calls that selfishness in them. Thus I once doubted those about me — not without reason in the beginning — and thus I once doubted you, Martin" (ch. 52); to wit, he doubts young Martin no more. Nonetheless, the "doubt" is an advance over the Nicholas-Cheeryble, Kit-Garland equations, as is the fact of young Martin's token trial in the swamps of Eden:

It was long before he fixed the knowledge of himself so firmly in his mind that he could thoroughly discern the truth; but in the hideous solitude of that most hideous place, with Hope so far removed, Ambition quenched, and Death beside him . . . reflection came . . . and so he felt and knew the failing of his life, and saw . . . what an ugly spot it was. . . . He made a solemn resolution that when his strength returned he would not dispute the point or resist the conviction, but would look upon it as an established fact, that selfishness was in his breast, and must be rooted out. . . . So low had Eden brought him. So high had Eden raised him up. (Ch. 33)

Daleski's comment on this is that "the strenuousness of the assertion here is reminiscent of that by which Oliver Twist's virtue is vindicated, and it similarly suggests that Dickens was not deeply concerned with what he was doing."[4] This seems to me a sudden and surprising collapse of discrimination. In the first place, we have seen that in *Oliver Twist* Dickens was, in fact, so "deeply concerned" as to falsify his vision and to subordinate it to the countering apparatus of the plot in order to vindicate Oliver. Secondly, Dickens' commitment to Oliver was so total as to rule out any critical distance whatsoever. In the case of young Martin, Dickens continues to be concerned; the concern, however, is mitigated and brought into focus through a new sense of distance. In an alien setting, young Martin is made to reflect upon his shortcomings and to acknowledge that his motives have been tainted. Nothing about Oliver is tainted. The continuing problem, of course, is that the rooting out of the taint is arbitrary, unrealized, extraneous to the novel's central action, and authorially managed. Dickens rather than Eden brings Martin both "so low" as well as raises him "so high." At the same time, to conflate young Martin with Oliver is to miss the reality of Dickens' advance.

CHAPTER 5

Dombey and Son:
The Critical Self-Image

After Kathleen Tillotson there is general critical agreement that *Dombey and Son* marks for Dickens a departure of major dimensions.[1] This departure, however, has usually been seen rather exclusively in terms of planning, design, and overall formal structure. Much of this derives from Dickens' well-known letter to Forster.[2] That with *Dombey and Son* Dickens demonstrates a new willingness and ability to organize experience around a single powerful conception is well-established and readily granted. Nevertheless, Dickens' advance in this novel over his previous fiction is not a matter exclusively of formal strength. In a crucial way Dickens' formal strengths issue from a more achieved and cohering social perception and self-assurance than was evidenced by the structures of the novels that went before, although deriving from the tensions of those structures.

Oliver Twist, Nicholas Nickleby, The Old Curiosity Shop, and *Martin Chuzzlewit* end with the rehabilitation of the antithetical surrogate and with the vindication of the martyred victim through such rehabilitation. Oliver, Nicholas, Kit, and Martin all move towards the father figure, who sanctions their goodness, substantiates that goodness through reward, and effectively subsumes them into an arbitrary ideal. Simultaneously, the denial to Smike and Nell of the position that ought to be theirs (Smike is Ralph's son, and Nell has a rich granduncle come to provide for her) is seen as a sacrifice. With Nell, Dickens moves to a position where the martyr is made to articulate an actively negative response to the pursuit of wealth. Yet, Dickens' self-distrust in *The Old Curiosity Shop* is evidenced by his inability to avoid suffusing Nell with a pity that she herself neither feels nor demands. In *Martin Chuzzlewit* the obsession of Nell's grandfather with wealth is seen as the obsession of an entire culture. But old Martin, despite his bad temper, remains a *deus ex machina*, and young Martin, despite the taint in his motivations, finds his reward. *Dombey and Son* begins where *Oliver Twist, The Old Curiosity Shop*, and *Martin Chuzzlewit* end.

All the reversals of the earlier patterns are predicated upon Dickens' new perception — or the new courage of his old perception — of the Brownlow figure. Having explored in *Martin Chuzzlewit* the causal implications of money for morality, Dickens is now able to give us a Brownlow as he might be within the actualities of the mid-Victorian mercantile culture, without insistence on the mythic. Since the making of money is now seen to be antithetical to a human ethic — Ralph, Gride, Nell's grandfather, the Brasses, were the tentative presentations here, all neutralized by the countering good rich men — Brownlow, divested of the wishful, must in essence be Dombey. Brownlow's goodness continues to be projected, but in severance now from his power. Relegated to obscurity by the dominant mercantile values of the culture, the discovery of the human strength of the Cuttle figure and the making of that strength available to the culture in increasingly integrated and organic dramatic formulations defines the nature of Dickens' idealism and art from here on. The culminating point in this process will no doubt be Joe Gargery. Having brought himself to revise his understanding of the Brownlow figure, Dickens is now able to initiate a more honest and self-assured adjustment to his ideological problematic, to see the victimized self-image in a new perspective and put it to a new and more critical use.

Philip Collins asks, "What does the Dombey firm produce or trade in?" and answers that Dickens "is making a traditional moral point about pride and riches, not a specifically nineteenth-century one about a particular economic system."[3] Henri Talon in a more recent evaluation agrees with Collins and goes further toward denying *Dombey and Son* any historical locus: "*Dombey and Son* has a kinship with moralizing allegories and even with fairy tales."[4] This insistence on reducing Dickens to fairy tale betrays in itself an ideology and is guilty of the same deviousness or, at least, the same willful ignorance that Peter Laurie of the British Parliament showed in the face of *Oliver Twist*: the honorable member thought Jacob's Island a fairy-tale figment of Dickens' imagination. And we know what Dickens had to say about that. Now, it is a reliable generalization that Dickens' outrage against the ills of his culture is consistently a moral outrage; at the same time, it is nonsense to suggest that Dickens was unaware of or unconcerned with the particular historical imperatives of nineteenth-century England, even with the decade-to-decade transformations in socioeconomic and political realities. *Household Words, All the Year Round,* and the *Letters* are a record of Dickens' changing and developing responses to the dynamics of his culture. Dickens was intensely cognizant of the fact that the conflict between the rich and the poor had acquired in his time a character and a significance which did not obtain before and which threatened to destroy England as a moral entity. Thus, writing to Burdett-Coutts in support of Austen Henry Layard, whom Burdett-Coutts had accused of fomenting unrest, Dickens says:

I differ from you altogether, as to his setting class against class. He finds them already set in opposition. And I think you hardly bear in mind that as there are two great classes looking at each other in this question, so there are two sides to the question itself. You assume that the popular class take the initiative. Now as *I* read the story, the aristocratic class did that . . . and it is *they* who have put *their* class in opposition to the country—not the country which puts itself in opposition to them.[5]

As for the middle class, Dickens sees it now as "a poor fringe on the mantel of the upper."[6] In "That Other Public" and "The Great

Baby," for example, Dickens speaks specifically to the question of corruption in big business (since *Dombey and Son* is about big business) and in government, as well as to the alliance between them in their common strategy to treat the masses as ignorant and infantile fodder.[7] Yet more specifically related to *Dombey and Son* is Dickens' attack, in *Household Words* and *All the Year Round*, on the role of money, on wealthy directors of companies who owe their positions exclusively to their wealth, on fraudulent and exploitive financial practices, even on profitable approaches to bankruptcy, on members of the railway board who vote down safety devices, on the practice of allowing officers in the army to buy their commissions (officers like Joe Bagstock, whose prescriptions for solving the problem of the poor is to "shoot the beggars through the head" [ch. 27]).[8] Speaking to the Metropolitan Sanitary Association in 1850 of the "contrasts of rank," "great contrasts of wealth and great contrasts of comfort," Dickens observes that "no such contrasts as were afforded by our handsome streets, our railroads and our electric telegraphs, in the year of our Lord 1850, as compared with the great mass of the dwellings of the poor in many parts of this metropolis [have] ever before been presented on this earth."[9] Clearly, all these statements about nineteenth-century England, in and around "the year of our Lord 1850," are hardly "allegories" or "fairy tales."

Dombey and Son belongs to the period (1843–50) when Dickens' distrust of England's bourgeois parliament as well as of the trading class begins to become total, the attendant irony being that in everything Dickens says from now on he sees himself not as one of the exploited for whom he speaks but as a success within the culture he seeks to reprove. Dickens' endeavor from *Dombey and Son* onward is to come to grips with that irony and that contradiction — one might even say, to atone for the urgencies that dictated the paranoid and arbitrary resolutions of the fiction hitherto. All the while, his increasing distance from and criticism of his culture is also a distance from and a criticism of himself. This is the process that leads his art out of the earlier amalgam of shrill denunciation and broken though self-rewarding sentiment toward the more even and critical structures of the fiction to come, beginning with *Dombey and Son*.

One has only to compare Dickens' presentation of the "offices of Dombey and Son" with the perfunctory and wholly undefined and unplaced descriptions of Brownlow's, Ralph's, and Quilp's professions to see why it is that *Dombey and Son* conveys in its totality a sure sense of the relentlessness of mid-Victorian commercialism:

The offices of Dombey and Son were within the liberties of the city of London, and within hearing of Bow Bells. . . . Gog and Magog held their state within ten minutes' walk; the Royal Exchange was close at hand; the Bank of England, with its vaults of gold and silver . . . was their magnificent neighbour. Just round the corner stood the rich East India House. . . . Anywhere in the immediate vicinity there might be seen pictures of ships speeding away full sail to all parts of the world; outfitting warehouses ready to pack off anybody anywhere fully equipped in half an hour. (ch. 4)

Not only does Dickens tell us what Dombey trades in ("hides," not "hearts"), but he also does something more embracing; he presents an evocative picture of an entire world of banking, new finance, and imperial expansion, and places the firm of Dombey and Son squarely in its middle. The close and rushed huddling together of the specified godlike institutions of the "city of London," the ships, the warehouses, and the silver and gold in the bank vaults creates through powerful evocation the total preoccupation of all England — "trade." Carker, the "new man," a "forerunner of the managerial revolution,"[10] tells Edith, "We have partnerships of interest and convenience, friendships of interest and convenience, dealings of interest and convenience, marriages of interest and convenience, every day" (ch. 45). Dombeyism is presented in terms which one recognizes to be prophetic of the modern world of corporate capital. One might go further and venture that in associating Major Bagstock — who "is wealthy . . . truly military," and who has done "active service" in the "Peninsula" and in "the East and West Indies" (ch. 10) — with Dombey, Dickens in some way anticipates our military-industrial complexes. Far-fetched, perhaps, but potentially there.

When Dombey is constrained to hire Polly Toodle — a "deserving object" (ch. 2) — as a wet nurse for Paul, he "desire[s] to make it a question of wages altogether." Hence, Dombey makes clear that "It is not at all in this bargain that you need become attached to my child, or that my child need become attached to you. I don't expect or desire anything of the kind. Quite the reverse. When you go away from here, you will have concluded what is a mere matter of bargain and sale, hiring and letting: and will stay away. The child will cease to remember you and you will cease, if you please, to remember the child" (ch. 2). The arrangement with Polly whereby she is to supply mother's milk to keep Son alive is seen purely as a contract between employer and employee. In order to obliterate Polly's identity totally, to assign her a functional, market tag, Dombey declares that she will during the term of the contract be Richards, not Polly. Podsnap-like, Dombey disposes of reality with edict; Gradgrind-like, he shames emotion by force of sheer fact. In the present instance the fact reads thus: Paul is a Dombey, and Polly, indigent labor; hence the nourishment she supplies is to be viewed as duly purchased merchandise. In this whole interaction between Dombey and Polly Toodle, Dickens shows a clear understanding of the particular modalities — especially of the relations of production — along which capitalism functions. In Polly's contractual position he sees the reified commodity status of labor, and in her transmutation from Polly to Richards he makes the point about alienation both along capitalist and sexist lines. The episode uses the very terms Marx and Engels are going to use — "wages," "hiring," "contract," "bargain and sale," and so forth. More significantly, and poignantly, Dickens sees the tragic division between feeling and function that is enforced by the new economic system. Polly is not to get *attached* to Paul; that is not part of the contract. The concentrated ironies of this whole first part of the novel derive, I think, from Dickens' ability to underscore, to enact, the history-making significance of Dombey's insistence on applying the terms and categories of commercial life to private reality. Dickens here has a marvelous hold of the inauguration of a new *episteme*. In the case of Polly Toodle, Dickens is especially able to produce the most stark irony: it is life, literally, that Polly is to give to the infant. And, of course, in the social-historical dimension of the situation, life, after all, does flow from labor to the capitalist.

Dombey's insistence on always quashing the purely human interchange between people is what lends him his status as death. Dickens surrounds Dombey with funereal imageries and a funereal ethos and unambiguously establishes him as the cause of the general "blight": "When he looked out . . . at the trees in the little garden, their brown and yellow leaves came fluttering down, as if he blighted them" (ch. 5). The context here is that of Paul's so-called christening, which, Dickens tells us, is more akin to a funeral in every way except for the color of the coach. Dombey is shown as alienated from nature (his house is emblematic of him in having two sooty, leafless, gaunt trees outside it), from other human beings, and finally from himself. Dickens provides an image of Dombey's self-alienation early in chapter 3; the perspective is Polly Toodle's, but clearly, we are meant to share it: "From the glimpses she caught of Mr. Dombey at these times, sitting in the dark distance . . . she began to entertain ideas of him in his solitary state, as if he were a lone prisoner in a cell, or a strange apparition that was not to be accosted or understood." At the very start of the novel, the prisoner image allows Dickens to capture the paradoxical impotence of Dombey's entire system of assertion and to prepare grounds for its overthrow.

Meanwhile, the paramount consideration before Mr. Dombey is that "this young gentleman [Paul] has to accomplish a destiny" (ch. 1). All surrounding reality must be made to serve only that end. Dickens establishes the context of that destiny early in the chapter: "The earth was made for Dombey and Son to trade in, and the sun and moon were made to give them light. Rivers and seas were formed to float their ships; rainbows gave them promise of fair weather; winds blew for or against their enterprises; stars and planets circled in their orbits, to preserve inviolate a system of which they were the centre." This is not the allegory of one man's pride and riches, as Collins contends. The operative pronoun throughout is plural. The "system" of which Dombey and Son are the center is the mid-Victorian system of "enterprises." Given the central placement of the offices of Dombey and Son within the bulwarks of British commerce, Paul's destiny is the very destiny of England; of this destiny Kipling is to be the laureate and high priest. The "stars and planets" might indeed be the colonies, whose only *raison d'être* lies in their contribution to the ever-lasting glory of Britannia. The "sun never sets" over Britannia be-cause she is the "light" of the world. Any reckless Galileo who might suggest that the world does not revolve around Dombey and Son must either be ignored, or bought, or stamped out (Flor-ence, Polly and Alice, Edith and Carker). Dickens' concentrated indictment in *Hard Times* of the fractured and fracturing philosophy of utility finds its first major expression here, not only in terms of its emotional bankruptcy but, as Raymond Williams shows, in terms of Dickens' perception of the human and social consequences of the alliance between institutionalized empiricism and the requirements of a class: as I said earlier, Gradgrind's daugh-ter is reserved for Bounderby.[11]

It is this perception, I think, that helps to explain the signifi-cance of Dickens' ambivalence toward the railways in *Dombey and Son*.[12] Insofar as the railways help to "let the light of day in on" the "miserable habitations far below" (ch. 20), insofar as they originate "wholesome comforts and conveniences" in old slum areas and lead to "villas, gardens, churches, healthy public walks" (ch. 15) and raise the subsistence of the Toodles, the railways are good. But, insofar as the railways project a mechanistic, abstract power, "tearing on" resistless (ch. 20) and swallowing up, overnight, Staggs' Gardens, a morsel to the "monster" (ch. 15), the railways portend no good and point to *Hard Times*. The sophisticated complexity of Dickens' position is suggested quite curiously: he ends a totally negative presentation of the railways — "the first shock of a great earthquake" — with a positive statement, that the railroad "trailed smoothly away, upon its mighty course of civilization and im-provement" (ch. 6); and later, in chapter 15, a wholly positive ac-count of the same railroad with a negative statement: "But Staggs' Gardens had been cut up root and branch. Oh woe the day! when 'not a rood of English ground' — laid out in Staggs' Gardens — is secure!" Although ideologically inconsistent, Dickens captures imaginatively the human consequences of this new power and sug-gests them through sure art. The logic of the attendant emotion proceeds somewhat like this: Polly Toodle suckles Paul; Polly Too-dle lives in Staggs' Gardens; the railways uproot Staggs' Gardens; the railways cannot be good. When Dombey travels by train to

Leamington, thinking through the entire journey about Paul's death, the narrative, poised with a new subtlety between external and internal perception, focuses with remorseless insistence on the train as "Death" (ch. 20). Again, in chapter 42, Dombey tells Carker that "the idea of opposition to Me is monstrous and absurd." The spirit of Dombeyism (the abstract and monomaniacal "Me") is also the spirit that propels, without thought of "opposition," the "monster train" (ch. 15). This identity is grimly established through Carker's death. Opposing Dombey, Carker is crushed by the train. The art in all this demonstrates Dickens' clearest insight yet into the quality of the human impetus behind the Industrial Revolution. It also suggests how the railways may directly be related to the premises upon which Dombey deals with the world. Thus, Polly's transformation into Richards adumbrates the annihilation of Staggs' Gardens by the railways. Thus, the railways — the power of wealth translated into steel — work centrally with the persistent imagery of chill, lack of "heart," and unyielding posture which has been often written about.

This new clarity and forthrightness about the shaping forces of Dickens' culture and their human implications generate in *Dombey and Son* from the beginning its sureness of direction, detail, and tone.[13] Two major, interlocking reversals take place at the outset. First, unlike the victims in the earlier novels, Paul is born into the class, status, and wealth which Dickens seeks for Oliver throughout that novel and gives him at the end. Secondly, unlike the previous novels, *Dombey and Son* presents the situation, not of the child-victim seeking the father figure, but of the father seeking the sanctioning son (without a son Dombey and Son faces extermination). The case of Florence might suggest otherwise, yet, in actuality, the new pattern holds true in her case at a deeper conceptual level; Dombey and Son will turn out "a daughter after all." Whereas Dombey needs Son for the salvation of Dombey and Son, he needs Florence for his salvation as a human being. Thus, it is not Florence (Cordelia) who must discover Dombey (Lear) but vice versa. Paul and Florence are to be seen together as they resurrect Dombey severally, Paul critically and Florence through sheer staying power. For the half of this composite image that is vested in Paul it is, ironically, the dependence of the father which becomes the problem (because the dependence is not on son but on Son), a problem which Paul, as martyr, resolves, once again, through death. For the other half, Florence, the father's refusal to depend becomes the source of pain. That refusal she meets, in a battle of attrition, with a withering patience. To Paul, the martyr, Dickens now gives a new self-assurance (issuing from the self-assurance that enables Dickens now to see Dombey without illusion) and a new critical intelligence. Accordingly, Paul's function is to undermine not just Dombey but Dombeyism through his sharp, disconcerting precocity. Dombey's inability, through the action of the novel, to find adequate answers to Paul's questions then becomes a condition of his finding Florence.

Dombey's treatment of Polly Toodle, as I suggested earlier, clearly establishes the ruling terms and tenets of Dombeyism. Artistically, this major juxtaposition between the worlds of Dombey and Toodle in the novel also contains within itself the necessary condition of the projected fall of Dombey. The life-giving succor for Paul, the Son, comes from the lower orders. Having purchased life for Paul, Dombey throws Polly out at the first pretext that offers itself. Paul, on the other hand, senses that the "old-fashioned" void in his life requires Polly and Florence to stay by him. Appropriately, therefore, Paul's question about money, setting up the central resonance of the novel's experience, comes immediately after Polly has been discharged.

Dombey and Son have been quiet. Suddenly, Paul breaks "silence thus: Papa! what's money?" Mr. Dombey, who is "quite disconcerted,"

would have liked to give him some explanation involving the terms circulating-medium, currency, depreciation of currency, paper, bullion, rates of exchange . . . and so forth; but looking down at the little chair, and seeing what a long way down it was, he answered: "Gold, and silver, and copper. Guineas, shillings, half-pence. You know what they are?"

"Oh yes, I know what they are," said Paul. "I don't mean that, Papa. I mean what's money after all?" (ch. 8)

What is money, after all? While an amazed Dombey, clearly out of his depth, considers Paul's poser about essence, Paul presses further: "I mean, Papa, what can it do?" Reassured somewhat by the more practical nature of Paul's secondary query, Dombey returns, "Money, Paul, can do anything." "Anything, Papa?" "Yes. Anything—almost." "Why didn't money save me my Mama?" the child asks finally. The point that Dickens is making here is indeed a profound one. Two opposed and irreconcilable kinds of speculation are presented. The speculations that characterize Dombeyism are truly not speculations but calculations grounded solidly on the reality of lucre. That is the one sure assumption of the Dombey world. Paul's countering speculation, however, is a philosophical, even religious, speculation about essence and existence: can the power of money be "real" if it cannot save life? Indeed, how "real" is life itself? And if life itself is in essence "unreal," then the countables of the Dombey world cannot but be pitiful illusions. Marvelously, the roles of the child and the adult are reversed. Dombey is the child for whom shape, color, and form are real and for whom silver and gold have substance; Paul is lifted, on the other hand, to a height from which he can sense the world to be a shadow world, the domain of terribly ignorant and terribly proud people. This must be the realization in Paul that makes the child turn to the world of dream, of forms and visions that are not solid but float on water and recede long distances in time and space with the fluid but endless sea.

Having perceived with a "child's quickness" that he has already made his father "uncomfortable," Paul withdraws and wonders to himself, being his own best audience. Dickens is able to create a strangely and rather ominously evaluative critical distance between father and son. The keenly attentive novelist sums up:

Mr. Dombey was so astonished, and so uncomfortable, and so perfectly at a loss how to pursue the conversation, that he could only sit looking at his son by the light of the fire, with his hand resting on his back, as if it were detained there by some magnetic attraction. Once he advanced his other hand, and turned the contemplative face towards his own for a moment. But it sought the fire again as soon as he released it; and remained, addressed towards the flickering blaze, until the nurse appeared, to summon him to bed.

"I want Florence to come for me" said Paul. (ch. 8)

With Paul, Dickens, in making himself ask *the* question, achieves a veritable rite of passage. The force of Nell's option for poverty, we remember, is betrayed by a redundancy of authorial sympathy — sympathy that issues from resentment rather than from conviction and suggests a lack of nerve. Having exhausted himself with Nell, Dickens realizes in Paul a disturbing and sustained sharpness of critical focus on the central problem of his culture. Unlike Oliver, Smike, Nell, Nicholas, and Kit, Paul in his questioning seeks to subvert the fundamental cultural assumptions of Dombeyism. Having rendered masterfully the Dombey doctrine, Dickens then suggests his own complete intellectual control by the unrelenting thrust of Paul's interrogatives and the assimilation of their implications into the life of the novel. The "abrupt question" finds Dombey "astonished," "uncomfortable," "alarm[ed]," and "perfectly at a loss how to pursue the conversation." Dombey, made to wonder for the first time about the validity of his life values, is transfixed in a bewilderment in which the more he seeks to establish the rightful power of money, the more surely he comes across as arguing the bankruptcy of an entire culture. All he can do is stare at Paul in "magnetic attraction." On his part, Paul's rejection of his father's system of reality is firmly conveyed in his turning away from Dombey's dead and cold world of "guineas, shillings, halfpence" towards the "fire." The resolution of this debate on value (a resolution that foreshadows the movement of the novel's whole experience) comes firmly from Paul: "I want Florence to come for me." In chapter 10, when Walter and Cuttle come to Dombey to seek aid for Sol Gills, Dombey promptly seizes the situation to make an example of it to Paul, whose question has not ceased to rankle him: "You see, Paul . . . how powerful money is, and how anxious people are to get it. Young Gay comes all this way to *beg* for money, and you, who are so grand and great, having got it, are going to let him have it, as a great favour and obligation." Would Paul, then, "*lend* it to his old Uncle . . . ?" "'*Give* it to his old Uncle,' returned Paul" (emphasis added). The trenchant sureness of value that Paul evidences in his judgmental questioning of his father is then, significantly, carried immediately to the sphere of education. When Mrs. Pipchin asks Paul, with complacent self-regard, "How do you think you shall like me?" Paul's answer is, "I don't think I shall like you at all" (ch. 8). This interchange is charged with an intensity that makes the loud melodrama between Nicholas and Squeers seem mere puppetry. Paul was "not fond of her; he was not afraid of her": this new ability of the self-image to bring not only the surrounding context but also itself into distanced perspective, without any accompanying gush, is a measure of how far Dickens has traveled with *Dombey and Son*.

Paul's question releases the force that leads, through a cumulative process of interaction and disillusionment, to the crash of Dombey and Son. The question is kept alive and adroitly orchestrated through the span of the novel's action. On the journey to Leamington, not long after Paul's death, Dombey, brooding over "the impotence of his will, the instability of his hopes," could "hardly forbear inquiring, himself, what *could* [money] do indeed: what had it done?" (ch. 20). As the Dombey house is altered in anticipation of Dombey's acquiring another Mrs. Dombey, Dombey observes, "All that money could do, has been done, I believe." Clearly, Dombey now implies that there are certain things money may *not* do — an implication which is sharply heightened by Cleopatra's question, "And what can it not do, dear Dombey?" The following context immediately offers an answer: "Nothing that his wealth could do, though it were increased ten thousand fold, could win him for its own sake, one look of softened recognition from the defiant [Edith] . . . arrayed with her whole soul against him" (ch. 35). The climactic point of this movement is dramatized when Edith plucks the "tiara of bright jewels" from her head, "cast[s] the gems upon the ground," and "look[ing] on Mr. Dombey to the last," walks out on Dombeyism (ch. 47). Consistent with the parallel structure defined by Mrs. Skewton and Edith on the one side, and Mrs. Brown and Alice on the other (a parallel that has received much comment), the repudiation by Edith is followed by a more humiliating repudiation by Edith's counterpart in London's lower orders, Alice. Come to get what "intelligence" he can "in a hovel like this," Dombey offers money in the arrogant belief that, at least, where it concerns such scum as Alice and her mother money "will bring about unlikely things." His offer is met by Alice's ringing question, "Do you know nothing more powerful than money?" (ch. 52), a question that reinforces all previous experience of the book. Finally, after the crash and the reconciliation, Dombey "would repeat that . . . question, 'What is money?' and ponder on it, and think about it, and reason with himself . . . for a good answer; as if it had never been proposed to him until that moment" (ch. 61).

Finally, one can see what a finely sustained dual — and opposed — movement Dickens carries through the whole novel: one, the linear movement of positivist history, captured centrally in the symbol of the railroad that rushes mindlessly on; and the other, a reverse movement of introspection in which, as Dombey wishes to rush forward, he is constantly obliged to go backward to make an assessment of scenes and situations that he must understand in order to come to a reliable comprehension of his total reality. Thus, contrary to his posture that Florence simply does not exist, Dombey chafes inwardly at the memory of the clasp between Florence and her dying mother — an experience, a communion from which, we recall, he feels wretchedly "quite shut out" (ch. 3). Dombey must, in his own mind, however furtively, return to what Florence means, just as he must, time and again, return to Paul's question about money. Dickens' purpose is subtle, and indicative of the ideological position he is to take increasingly in relation to any version of historical determinism. It is to show that no mechanical forward lunge in time can, or need, be automatically "progressive" unless history and time are constantly enriched by introspection. Dombey's recuperation is in this sense dearly earned — in contradiction to what Taine and other critics of his persuasion feel about the novel's conclusion.

Although the old problem of martyrdom remains ("The light about the head is shining on me as I go!" [ch. 16]), Paul, as thesis, marks a great advance over Dick, Oliver, Smike, and Nell. In contrast to Dickens' problem with Nell — how to bring himself to kill her off — Dickens' resolute design with respect to Paul must indeed seem ruthless: "When the boy is about ten years old . . . he will be taken ill, and will die." A little later: "Paul I shall slaughter at the end of number five . . . all I *have* written is point."[14] The "point" now consists in making Paul's early death critically functional toward Dickens' stronger purpose of dramatizing Dombey and his fall. As a shaping human influence Paul is kept alive in Florence, who, through her long-suffering patience (although hardly a rendered suffering), vindicates Paul, as son, after Dickens has purposefully slaughtered him as Son.[15]

Given the conceptual design behind Dickens' thesis and his more evolved treatment of that thesis, one can see the significance of his initial purpose with respect to Walter Gay. Dickens wrote to Forster: "About the boy, who appears in the last chapter of the first number, I think it would be a good thing to disappoint all the expectations that chapter seems to raise of his happy connection with the story and the heroine, and to show him gradually and naturally trailing away . . . into negligence, idleness, dissipation, dishonesty and ruin. To show how good turns into bad, by degrees."[16] "To show how good turns into bad by degrees": this is indeed a long way from *Oliver Twist*, where Dickens' purpose was in part to present Oliver as the "principle of good" unaffected by "adverse circumstance." Having differentiated Brownlow into Dombey, Dickens can see that to show Walter making good would be to reduce, mitigate, and falsify his new perception and the very point of his attack. Dickens' statement about Walter, then, is his first conscious criticism of Oliver, Nicholas, and Kit. Formulating as he is now a moral, idealist synthesis, Dickens is able to see at the outset that for Walter the point of arrival ought to be not Dombey but Gills and Cuttle (as Joe will be for Pip). The mediating figures of Esther, Louisa Gradgrind, and Amy Dorrit clearly show Dickens working toward that synthesis — toward images that will neither escape into or be rewarded with death nor vindicated through money, but will be obliged to be implicated in and to suffer, over protracted periods of time, the imperatives of the Dombey world. Whereas his misgivings about Walter are evidence of a high point of perception and adjustment, his final acquiescence ("for reasons that need not be dwelt upon"), his conscious compromise, becomes so much more damning.[17] After Walter Gay, however, the Dickens' antithesis becomes vestigial and is dropped. The surrogate images coalesce, and the more painful (and more dramatized) process of adult confrontation begins. The first point of that process is David, who must come to grips with himself and, therefore, tell his own story.

CHAPTER 6

David Copperfield:
The Price of Success

I

Criticism of *David Copperfield*, often referred to as Dickens' "most personal book,"[1] after the well-known sentiment of Dickens' own later Preface, has been generally colored by a rather lush empathy—the critic's willingness to surrender to David's self-extenuating voice. The complacence with which the touching teleology of David's arrival (to Agnes) has been accepted is, in my view, a fine instance of our ideological collusion with David—and, in part, with Dickens. The impulsion here has been to sweep the disconcerting, even the sly, under the carpet as something "mistaken."[2] This has been achieved by emphasizing David's emotional life— by which I mean, specifically, his relationship with the women in the novel—and by treating all other interactions as a stratum of subsidiary life, or as something to be understood only in relation to the primary business of David's romantic illuminations (from Emily to Dora to Agnes). Thus, this personal and poetic treatment—and the significant neglect of the social and the moral —has encouraged a predictable drawing of parallels with Wordsworth's *Prelude* and Carlyle's *Sartor Resartus* as kindred enactments of epiphanic becoming. Simultaneously, the psychoanalytic industry has found rich material in the other women (Clara, Peggotty, Mrs. Micawber, Betsy Trotwood, who together make up the composite mother figure), as David's oedipal longing has been seen to condition and excuse his "mistaken" impulses.

How far Gwendolyn Needham's benign reading of David's career — the acquiring of "discipline" by a "man of sensibility" who has "innocence, simplicity, gullibility, benevolence, tenderness"—has set the tone for much subsequent criticism, I shall suggest as I proceed. Yet the evidence shows that, wittingly or unwittingly, Needham has succeeded all too well in diverting us from the less innocent aspects of David's *Bildungsroman*, directing our attention away from an evaluation of David's moral intelligence by fixing it on a process of melioration that is calculated to obscure the critical problematic in the novel. In the process "discipline" is given the most hopelessly private and facile definition and effectively detached from social obligation, from the internally substantiated claims of urgent human commitment. "David's is the story," we are told, "of the Self as moral survivor."[3] This is indeed begging the question: *does* David, after all, survive morally? What sort of "hero" (ch. 1) is he?[4] What view *can* we take of his heroism? How does Dickens now see the matter? And, can we say that Dickens is in full control of David's narrative, and able or willing to step back with equal readiness in all contexts? What can we deduce from the degree and the quality of the Dickens-David equation about the ongoing Dickens dialectic?

II

Between *Dombey and Son* and *David Copperfield* falls the fragment of autobiography that Dickens sent Forster.[5] It is well to recall, therefore, that the intention behind that fragment was, as Dickens told Forster, to recapitulate painful details in order to face and understand the traumatic formative experiences that "have worked together to make me what I am,"[6] experiences that Dickens had not disclosed before, even to his wife. Clearly, Dickens in 1849–50, at the "pinnacle of fame,"[7] assured of his place, felt that it was time to "take stock of the past."[8] Yet, Dickens' willingness to be overtly personal at this stage has its curious counterpoint, something that makes sense if we keep in mind his preceding explorations. As we know, Dickens abandoned the autobiography; however, when Forster suggested that the new book be written in the first person, Dickens took readily to the suggestion.[9] Lucas argues that Dickens opted for the new narrative form in order to be "inside his hero."[10] It is obvious that many details of David's life (including passages quite literally lifted out of the autobiographical fragment and incorporated into the novel — see chapter 11 of *David Copperfield*) make David a very personal presentation, if that is what Lucas means. Yet, the significance of this new mode of narration seems to me to point in exactly the opposite direction from Lucas's suggestion: having posited Dick, Oliver, Smike, Nell, and Paul with the angry energy of an unqualified emotional and social commitment, Dickens, in letting David tell his own story is, in effect, creating for the first time a space between the direct force of his formative experience and the terms of its transference into art. David, the successful author, who watches the hurt little child grow up is watched in turn by Dickens and the reader. As a protagonist who struggles with his past and who is obliged now to grow out of a childhood hallowed by Dickens, the narrator's intelligence now functions inside the created world of the novel and is made answerable.[11] The "blank center" begins to fill in with shades of grey. With the earlier self-images the reader has only the option of total empathy: those who fail to see the action of *Oliver Twist, Nicholas Nickleby, The Old Curiosity Shop, Dombey and Son* with Dick, Oliver, Smike, Nell, and Paul share, in effect, in Dickens' indictment of the ills these books present. In his work before *David Copperfield* Dickens offers little freedom of intervention. In that critical sense, then, those are the books that are wholly personal. As Dickens lives out the direct but crippling energy of that phase and acquires a place in his own culture (an irony central to the dialectic of his growth), he is, with *David Copperfield*, willing to remove himself from the charged urgencies that inform the earlier work. David neither dies a valorized child nor finds the saving Brownlow (Betsy Trotwood goes broke, so that David must cut his own way through a "forest of difficulty" [ch. 37]); Oliver's story, in a sense, ends with

David's arrival at Dover. From there on Oliver must grow up and fight his own battles, as well as forge his own priorities. He must now suffer the pain of adult confrontation, both with his own past and with the people with whom he is to interact. There remains an authorial screen around David, but the scars of the confrontation begin to be visible. The emotional scars David sees and heightens only too readily, but the moral damage they cause him he does not either fully recognize or admit. Nonetheless, this damage colors some of David's relationships and defines the quality of his humanity (in relation, for example, to the Micawber family, Traddles, the Peggottys). In turn, the authorial attempt to muffle this damage, to provide David the tone of a special pleading, defines Dickens' failure in *David Copperfield*. Dickens, nevertheless, is not altogether able to control our response to the indulgent texture of the narrative in certain crucial contexts or able to limit for us the ugly implications of certain patterns that bear reflexively upon David (in relation, for example, to Uriah Heep). There is thus a tension between the moral thrust of the narrative and the limiting counterthrust of the author-narrator. And the critical enterprise ought to be to push the self-clarification of the narrative further into the open from under the camouflage contrived in part by the narrator and in part by Dickens.

David Copperfield is a medial point of Dickens' distance from himself, a critically central *Bildungsroman* in which the education of the hero is left incomplete and in which social and moral questions are more open than closed, notwithstanding Agnes's pointing upward.[12] It is a point where Dickens begins to acknowledge, however painfully, a "sinful innocence"[13] which in *Great Expectations* translates to acknowledged guilt. A good case may already be made for the guilt—a guilt which, I suggest, extends beyond the scope of the instances that Spilka cites: the biting of Murdstones' hand, the death of Spenlow, the death of Dora. In the first of these instances there really is no problem of moral discordance: quite clearly we are with David. If anything, it is David's sense of guilt which seems to me phony. We share David's assessment of Spenlow's "stiff" *Gestalt* (ch. 23), and his death does not leave a powerful enough residue for either David or the reader to bother with much. As for Dora's death it is so well-timed a piece of authorial engineering that David can be held guilty only by indirection, although Carl Baudelin, in a fine piece of structural analysis, is able to include the circumstance of Dora's death within a fascinating substructure of "acceptable fantasy and intolerable fact."[14] This is not to say that Dora's death cannot but weigh heavily on David and on Dickens. Lucas's analysis of the rapid diversionary strategies (especially the emphasis on Steerforth's death) that Dickens employs to submerge the impact and the meaning of Dora's death seems to me, in this context, fully convincing.[15] Of course, whereas Lucas sees this as a high point of control, I see these strategies as the narrator's and the author's attempt to neutralize the moral and psychological thrust of the narrative experience.

David's problem with Steerforth, with Steerforth in relation to the Peggottys, with Traddles, with the Micawber family, and with Uriah Heep is of a more embedded character, and relates to the continuing Dickens problematic. Given David's hardly fine or subtle and consistently annoying focus on his own gentility, on his determination to climb the "ladder" of "success" (ch. 42),[16] and on "fame," which he at one point recommends to Steerforth (ch. 20), the demands of his drive generate in him responses and judgments which are snobbish, callously self-regarding, and morally forgetful — showing an inability or unwillingness to carry the lessons of his childhood to comparable situations in other people's lives, as I will try to show. At their darkest, these responses and judgments are violently vengeful, when David perceives the possibility that his own barely concealed wishfulness might find realization elsewhere. The darkness I talk about here is morally less innocuous than Kincaid suggests in his perceptive article.[17] Kincaid differentiates clearly the sheltering structure of fantasy that David creates for himself, but Kincaid's most severe indictment of David — that "he is simply unable to act in a real situation" — argues essentially a weak and, by inference, pitiable protagonist, rather than one who expresses attitudes and allegiances which are repugnant in an *active sense*.[18]

III

As I said before, the prevailing critical consensus — and it is at bottom, a class consensus — still appears to reflect Needham's reading of *David Copperfield* as to the kind and degree of rigor with which David is to be viewed. Justly enough, Needham states that "as David's feeling pervades, colors, and gives significance to the story, so the story in turn reveals David's character and traces his emotional growth." In the subsequent pages of Needham's presentation, however, the emotional growth takes precedence over character. Her case is further delimited when she offers the parallel with Tom Jones. Assuming that David, like Jones, has "innate goodness" and is "lovable as boy, youth, and man," Needham proceeds to show how David learns his share of prudence. The reference of this prudence — Needham's term, taken obligingly from David himself, is "discipline" (ch. 45) — is then restricted to David's *anagnorisis* about the "mistaken impulse" of his heart when he first fell for Dora. Needham traces the stages up to this recognition (chs. 16, 19, 36, 42, 45), holding crucial the complication of the Dr. Strong–Annie Strong–Jack Maldon triad. Needham argues that having been struck by Annie Strong's statement of how her aged husband first saved her from the mistaken impulse of her heart (her fascination for Maldon), David goes on from there to reflect on his own persistently immature emotional life and to discover that what he feels for Agnes is not brotherly affection but sexual love. Thus, David is able to realize the wrongness and the injustice of his whole attitude toward Agnes — whom he has forbidden from accepting Heep in marriage — and, finally, releases her to marry whomsoever she desires, adding that that one sentiment is expressed without any "alloy of self" (ch. 62). Needham concludes that "having thus proved his hero's disciplined heart, Dickens rewards him with Agnes's hand and life-long love."[19] In all this, that other novel that concerns David's relationships with Steerforth, Traddles, the Micawbers, the Peggottys, and Heep finds hardly a mention; yet such a mention as it does find is a critical giveaway. In saying that "at times [David's] loyalty is misplaced, his feeling misdirected, or mistaken," Needham places the crucial emphasis casually, as though in passing — "mistaken" rather than willed. David's attachment to Steerforth, his "erroneous valuation," is put down to "his need for loving approval"; that David "inevitably feels superior" to Traddles and "cannot comprehend [Traddles' and Sophy's] unselfish consideration for Sophy's preposterous family" is likewise not a matter important enough for pause or comment; nor is the fact that after Emily's ruin David's "friend's unworthiness elicits [in him] more tenderness than wisdom." Heep simply "provides the contrast of the bad heart." Needham also remarks with a neutral blandness that "David's economic progress is steady but love's progress is not so smooth"; she chooses, however, to focus on David's *lack* of discipline in "love's progress" rather than his "steady" discipline about his "economic progress." Needham, of course, has no interest in pursuing the social implications of those positions, or their implications for David's other relationships.

I have quoted extensively from Needham in order to present her case as fully as possible in her own words. Insofar as Needham seeks to relate the experience of the Annie-Strong-Maldon complication to the details of David's life with Dora, she helps to restore what had seemed a somewhat peripheral matter to a more central and meaningful attention. Nonetheless, the moment that such morally extenuating terms as "lack of discipline," "mistaken impulse," and "erroneous valuation" are extended to define the substance of David's interactions with some of the other people in his life, one either acquiesces unguardedly in the terms of perception David supplies or declares a willing enough endorsement of those terms. That David's evaluation of Steerforth is "erroneous" is hardly in doubt; the question is, what does it tell us about David that Steerforth continues to be the "noble spirit" (ch. 57) long, long after David has acquired his so-called discipline? Is there not perhaps a pattern — an unflattering pattern — to David's "mistaken" impulses more crucially related to his "steady" "economic progress" than Needham acknowledges? Should not David's climb up the "ladder" of "success" (ch. 42) oblige us to examine with particular strenuousness of detail how David comes off in his human interactions? It is time that we pay greater attention to David's discipline than to his lack of it, and to the particular allegiances that discipline dictates. Needham reminds us with pride that David "achieves an excellent scholastic record." The question is, at what price?

IV

Let us first look at the relationship between David and Steerforth, and include in that relationship Tommy Traddles, whom

David posits as a rather nondescript schoolmate (really, an object of condescension), but whose place in the narrative in various shared contexts is one of illuminating contrast to David. As a consequence, one of the approaches to an evaluation of David's social urges and moral intelligence is through Traddles' response to situations that include both David and Traddles. Traddles functions as reliable comment on David throughout *David Copperfield*. The critical force of such defenses of David as base themselves on his tender age and emotional insecurity is nullified when we remember that Traddles is only as old as David and also an orphan.

At Creakle's Salem House David finds himself carried before Steerforth, who is "very good-looking," "as before a magistrate." At their first "feast," their "royal spread," David's hand shakes "at the very thought of doing the honours of the feast." David begs Steerforth for the "favour of presiding" (ch. 6). Soon David discovers that Steerforth, sent by his mother to Salem House so that he can be "monarch of the place" (ch. 20), is "the one boy in the school on whom [Creakle] never ventured to lay a hand." And a good thing too, because Steerforth, on being "asked . . . how he would proceed" if Creakle did dare to discipline him, "dipped a match into his phosphorus-box on purpose to shed a glare over his reply, and said he would commence by knocking him down with a blow on the forehead." That this is no idle showmanship we know from the treatment Mr. Mell is to receive. When David thinks of Steerforth's "nice voice, and his fine face, and his easy manner, and his curling hair," he does not wonder that Miss Creakle is in love with this magnificent piece of aristocracy. As David recalls honestly enough, "the reason of my mind running on him" was that "he was a person of great power" (ch. 6). The immunity that David senses (and sees) about Steerforth is the immunity that derives from class. Now, my argument is that as David grows, allegedly, into an independence of mind, his view of Steerforth remains uncorrected, not because he fails to see as much as because he *chooses* not to see. Throughout his life David wishes nothing better than that he were Steerforth. If this is recognized, then there need be nothing "inscrutable" about David's "love for Steerforth."[20]

When David leaves Dr. Strong's school — having been "eminent and distinguished in that . . . world" — and travels from Canterbury to London, he schools himself to "speak extremely gruff" and "condescendingly." As he is made to resign his seat behind the box, David comments that this was his "first fall . . . in life." David is acutely disturbed by the consciousness that "nobody stood in any awe of me at all: the chambermaid being utterly indifferent to my opinions on any subject, and the waiter being familiar with me, and offering advice" (ch. 19). David's problem (Dickens' problem?) springs from what Cockshut correctly sees as his "curiously ambiguous class position."[21] Although he wishes to be Steerforth, David has the disconcerting sense that in actuality he is what Uriah Heep says he is, "a puppy with a proud stomach," and "always an upstart" (ch. 52). And by his own admission, "Heep knew me better than I knew myself" (ch. 42). With Heep, nonetheless, David can bring himself to be angrily and righteously superior, but every time that he is face to face with Steerforth's butler, Littimer, his resources simply dissolve: "I always *did* feel as if this man were finding me out" (ch. 28). I shall return to this later.

What of Tommy Traddles? "Poor Traddles" ("the most miserable of all the boys") held it as a "solemn duty" for the boys "to stand by one another." For this, as might be expected, "he suffered . . . on several occasions." On one particular occasion "Steerforth laughed in church, and the Beadle thought it was Traddles"; so Traddles, "despised by the congregation," was taken out and caned. Traddles, however, "never said who was the real offender, though he smarted for it." It was not, of course, to be expected that Steerforth, "bold" and "brave as a lion," would come forth and say "who was the real offender." All the same, Traddles surely "had his reward." "Steerforth said there was nothing of the sneak in Traddles, and we all felt that to be the highest praise." David's "we" has a reference which is effectually restricted to David only: "I could have gone through a good deal . . . to have won such a recompense." David's assumption is, of course, that Traddles himself could not but look at the matter in this light. That Traddles nonetheless retains an independent moral courage and judgment is borne out in the confrontation that follows immediately between Steerforth and the poorest (although the most humane) teacher at Salem House, Mr. Mell, who, David tells us, "had a liking for me" (ch. 7).

As poor Mr. Mell enters his classroom, the boys whirl about him, "mimicking his poverty, his boots, his coat, his mother, everything belonging to him that they should have consideration for." How much "consideration" is shown Mr. Mell by David and Traddles severally is soon painfully contrasted. But the fact that David should talk about "consideration" here and promptly enough have small difficulty in endorsing Steerforth's treatment of Mell, is, I suggest, an early and revealing example of the nature of David's equivocations. Traddles, who by David's own admission has known more pain than anyone else at Creakle's, underscores this equivocation and places the quality of David's sympathy. Mell's bewildered, outraged question is, "How can you do it to me, boys?" Steerforth, "lounging with his back to the wall, and his hands in his pockets," whistled at Mr. Mell.

"Silence, Mr. Steerforth!" said Mr. Mell.

"Silence yourself," said Steerforth, turning red. "Whom are you talking to?"

.   .   .

"If you think, Steerforth," said Mr. Mell, "that I am not acquainted with the power you can establish over any mind here"—he laid his hand, without considering what he did (as I supposed), upon my head—"or that I have not observed you, within a few minutes, urging your juniors on to every sort of outrage against me, you are mistaken."

"I don't give myself the trouble of thinking at all about you," said Steerforth, coolly; "so I'm not mistaken, as it happens."

"And when you make use of your position of favouritism here, sir," pursued Mr. Mell, with his lip trembling very much, "to insult a gentleman —."

"A what?—where is he?" said Steerforth.

Here somebody cried out, "Shame, J. Steerforth! Too bad!" It was Traddles; whom Mr. Mell instantly discomfited by bidding him hold his tongue.

—"To insult one who is not fortunate in life, Sir, and who never gave you the least offense, and the many reasons for not insulting whom you are old enough and wise enough to understand," said Mr. Mell, with his lip trembling more and more, "you commit a mean and base action. You can sit down or stand up as you please, sir. Copperfield, go on."

"Young Copperfield," said Steerforth, coming forward up the room, "stop a bit. I tell you what, Mr. Mell, once for all. When you take the liberty of calling me mean or base, or anything of that sort, you are an impudent beggar. You are always a beggar, you know; but when you do that, you are an impudent beggar."

Through this interchange David "could not help thinking . . . what a noble fellow" Steerforth was, and "how homely and plain Mr. Mell looked opposed to him." This notwithstanding Traddles' courageous "Shame, J. Steerforth! Too bad." As Creakle arrives on the scene and demands to know what it is all about, Steerforth dares Mell "deny" that he is a "beggar," or that "if he is not a beggar himself, his near relation's one." Mell continues to "pat [David] kindly on the shoulder" while he looks at Steerforth. Steerforth then reveals the damning fact that Mell's "mother lives on charity in an alms-house" (having obtained this information from none other than David himself). Mr. Mell, charged and convicted, admits that Steerforth is right, "without correction," and is duly dismissed from Salem House. "Once more" laying "his hand upon [David's] shoulder," Mell wishes that Steerforth were "anything rather than a friend . . . to any one in whom" Mell has "an interest." Mell's moving cautioning of David is, of course, only the first of several such cautionings. Traddles, as I try to show, never registers on David, and even Betsy Trotwood's and Agnes's admonitions are never admitted by him. One wonders what shape *David Copperfield* might have taken had Steerforth not died.

Now, David feels that he would be "unfriendly" and "undutiful" to Steerforth to show any "contrition" for Mr. Mell. Traddles, however, quite plainly suggests to Steerforth that he has "ill-used" Mr. Mell, "hurt his feelings, and lost him his situation." "His feelings are not like yours, Miss Traddles" (ch. 7), Steerforth jeers back. (On the eve of his visit to Yarmouth Steerforth makes a more complete and a more completely insensitive statement on the feelings of "that sort of people" [ch. 20].) "As to his situation — which was a precious one, wasn't it? — do you suppose I am not going to write home, and take care that he gets some money?" David "thought this intention very noble in Steerforth." Everyone was "extremely glad to see Traddles so put down, and exalted Steerforth . . . especially when he told us, as he condescended to do, that what he had done had been done expressly for us . . . and that he had conferred a great boon upon us by unselfishly doing it" (ch. 7).

David's choice as between Mr. Mell and Traddles on the one hand and Steerforth on the other is not an isolated choice. Its premise continues to inform David's valuations long after he has left Dr. Strong's "excellent school" and is independently set up as an articled clerk. While still at Creakle's, David is visited by Ham and Mr. Peggotty, who bring him a gift of oysters. Steerforth, singing a song in a "gay and light manner" which bore "a kind of enchantment with it," happens to come in upon the three and momentarily walks away. David is flustered and embarrassed; he calls out to Steerforth "in the desire to explain to him how I came to have such a friend as Mr. Peggotty" (a close enough adumbration of the *Gestalt* of Joe's visit to Pip in London). "'Aye, aye?' said Steerforth." David then tells us that Steerforth "carried a spell with him to which it was a natural weakness to yield, and which not many persons could withstand" (ch. 7).[22] Traddles, Peggotty, Betsy Trotwood, Agnes, and Rosa Dartle all seem quite able to "withstand" Steerforth's "spell"; Emily does not, and for reasons similar to those that make Steerforth irresistible to David: David wants to be a gentleman; "Em'ly wanted to be a lady" (ch. 21).

When David encounters Steerforth again in London after a lapse of years, he "glow[s] with pleasure to find" that Steerforth still looks upon him as his "property" (ch. 20). This proprietary interest leads to David's first pilgrimage to Highgate. While at Highgate David tells Steerforth about Mr. Peggotty's "very pretty little niece" and wishes Steerforth would visit Yarmouth with him. Steerforth thinks it may not be altogether without fun to see "that sort of people." Rosa Dartle (quite the most incisive presentation in the novel) inquires whether "that sort of people" are "really animals and clods, and beings of another order." Steerforth obliges with the following summation:

"Why, there's a pretty wide separation between them and us," said Steerforth, with indifference. "They are not to be expected to be as sensitive as we are. Their delicacy is not to be shocked, or hurt very easily. They are wonderfully virtuous, I dare say—some people contend for that, at least; and I am sure I don't want to contradict them—but they have not very fine natures, and they may be thankful that, like their coarse rough skins, they are not easily wounded."

Rosa Dartle, fully aware of the "fine natures" the Steerforths possess (and therefore tormented all the more by a passion for Steerforth that her own intelligence rebukes), retorts with a simulation of satisfaction that bristles with irony and reminds us of the world of Jane Austen:

"Really!" said Miss Dartle. "Well, I don't know, now, when I have been better pleased than to hear that. It's so consoling! It's such a delight to know that, when they suffer, they don't feel! Sometimes I have been quite uneasy for that sort of people; but now I shall just dismiss the idea of them, altogether."

This is indeed devastating. Rosa Dartle loves Steerforth and must find it very painful (for example, more painful than Traddles might find it) to be objective in her judgment of Steerforth; yet, she holds onto her judgment with the strength of a tough and ironic intellect. What of David, our prospective man of letters, whose business, really, ought to be to make more acute and reliable discriminations than ordinary mortals? He "believed that Steerforth had said what he had, in jest," and "expected him to say as much when . . . we were sitting before the fire." Clearly, the Mell episode has meant nothing to David. We soon find David saying, "I subscribed . . . with all my heart" when Mrs. Steerforth, who has forgotten David's name, points out how "generous and noble" Steerforth "always" is. David then notes with adulation what "a picture of comfort, full of easy-chairs, cushions, and footstools" Steerforth's room is (ch. 20).[23]

At Highgate David engages in "lessons"—riding, boxing, fencing, all the accouterments of the gentleman-to-be. But all this, strangely enough, is directed at the butler Littimer again: "I never could bear to show my want of skill before the respectable Littimer." In the meanwhile, Steerforth, who had "a dashing way . . . of treating me like a plaything," grows still more in David's esteem, David "admiring him more in a thousand respects." We cannot point to a single good reason for such increased admiration in David's narrative. The day of their departure for Yarmouth arrives and Steerforth declares, "Let us see the natives in their aboriginal condition." Having met and "charmed" little Emily, Steerforth voices to David his opinion of Emily's Ham: "That's rather a chuckle-headed fellow for the girl." Though David feels "a shock in this unexpected and cold" assessment, he is nonetheless convinced that "there is not a joy or sorrow, not an emotion, of such people, that can be indifferent to you. And I admire and love you for it, Steerforth, twenty times the more!" (ch. 21).

So David's boyhood sweetheart is seduced by the friend he adores. And it changes nothing: "I am not afraid to write that I never had loved Steerforth better. . . . I thought more of all that was brilliant in him, I softened more towards all that was good in him, I did more justice to the qualities that might have made him a man of a noble nature and a great name, than ever I had done in the height of my devotion to him." The self-reflexive inwardness of David's empathy seems to make Manheim's conclusion inescapable; Emily's situation seems clearly a case of vicarious rape: "I believed that if I had been brought face to face with him, I could not have uttered one reproach" (ch. 32).[24] After many vicissitudes, including Dora's death, David's grief when Ham and Steerforth are washed ashore dead is not for Ham (who, David had acknowledged with generous Steerforth-like condescension, had the "soul of a gentleman" [ch. 30]) but for Steerforth: "I mourned for him who might have won the love and admiration of thousands, as he had won mine long ago" (ch. 58). When all is said and done, Steerforth is still "the noble spirit" (ch. 57). And nobility, as we have seen, carries no objective reference in the narrative in relation to Steerforth except that of class.

I realize that I am perhaps quoting text with excessive insistence; yet, if the meaning of the David-Steerforth-Traddles context is to be understood, we must have this context before us in its fullness (rather than just the case of Little Emily). And the full context is ugly. When Agnes warns David against his "bad Angel," David is infuriated that Agnes should "judge" Steerforth "from what you saw of me the other night" (referring to the night of his "dissipation"). Agnes points out that she does "not judge him from what I saw of you the other night." "From what, then?" asks David. How does one judge Steerforth? "From many things — trifles in themselves, but they do not seem to me to be so, when they are put together. I judge him, partly from your account of him . . . and your character, and the influence he has over you" (ch. 25). And we remember that Agnes has hardly met Steerforth. If Agnes can judge Steerforth even from "your account of him," if Traddles sees through Steerforth as early as Salem House, if Rosa Dartle is aware, despite her tragic passion, of the "corruption of him" (ch. 56), if the context of what Agnes calls "trifles" bespeak Steerforth's rottenness, why will David refuse to "judge" Steerforth? Unless it is that David conflates Steerforth with his best idea or projection of himself. I think the text I have presented shows that he does. Steerforth is a surrogate, a point of arrival. Unfortunately (or fortunately), he is no longer Brownlow or Cheeryble; so much the worse for David. Dickens, with the new space between himself and the self-image, is now able to see much of this. That as late as chapter 57 Steerforth is still the "noble spirit" (after David has supposedly acquired "discipline") suggests, of course, how hard it is for Dickens to let go even in the face of the narrative. Clearly, Dickens *sees* Steerforth's rottenness; I do not think he acknowledges equally clearly David's culpability. The particular voice that Dickens gives David is calculated to mitigate rather than to invite reproof. Somehow, however enormous David's omissions or commissions, his tone begs endless accommodation. The presence of Traddles in the text, with his active adherence to human value despite the price in pain, makes it impossible to grant David the accommodation he seeks. The directions are, nevertheless, clear enough. Eugene Wrayburn, for example, will demonstrate what Steerforth must undergo to become acceptable. Steerforth's one twinge ("I wish to God I had had a judicious father these last twenty years" [ch. 22]), one which fails to prevent him from ruining Emily, will translate into a real moral confrontation in Wrayburn with respect to Lizzy Hexam.

V

Traddles figures centrally in yet another relationship — the one between him, David, and Micawber — and in that relationship he serves to underscore David's unpleasantly self-regarding and calculating moral intelligence.

In chapter 11 David meets the Micawbers of Windsor Terrace,

and notices at once that the Micawber house "was shabby like [Micawber] himself." Soon, however, David, lonely and neglected, becomes "quite attached to the family," and a friendship springs between him and "these people." At the prospect of the Micawbers having to move from London on account of financial problems, David is heartbroken because he "had been so intimate with them" and was "so utterly friendless without them" (ch. 12). Mrs. Micawber, who has never considered David a lodger but a friend, refuses, nonetheless, to take pecuniary advantage of that friendship even when the family is in a crisis. The Micawbers offer David family and friendship at the most unforgettably bleak time of his life.

And yet David's first self-absorbed anxiety as he enters Dr. Strong's school at Canterbury is caused by his embarrassed (and embarrassing) recollection of his past with the Micawbers: "My mind ran upon what [my schoolmates] would think, if they knew of my familiar acquaintance with the King's Bench Prison? Was there anything about me which would reveal my proceedings in connexion with the Micawber family?" (ch. 16). David's first act of condescension after he is lodged at the Wickfield's is to accept Uriah Heep's invitation to dinner in chapter 17, "sensible . . . of being entertained as an honoured guest." Unexpectedly, through the open door, David notices none other than good old Micawber, who is delighted to have a "valued friend turn up." David, however, very shaken by the encounter, feels differently: "I cannot say—I really cannot say—that I was glad to see Mr. Micawber there." Mr. Micawber's heartiness contrasts only too noticeably with David's uneasy and unendearing reserve, and David is "excessively anxious to get Mr. Micawber away." It is important to remind ourselves that in all this David's intention is not to be expiatory; it is, rather, to present a clean view of himself, to take credit for his honesty about a bad feeling. It is a stance that, in the end, expects us to understand David's side of the case. For example, we are somehow to see that Micawber *is* shabby, that nobody *could* be glad to see him or feel guilt about wishing to see the back of him. It is in this that David's narrative falls short of Pip's and obliges us to be on guard—if we will. David's acute discomfort about and concealment of the Windsor Terrace days

is juxtaposed with Micawber's uninhibited frankness about his social difficulties: "I have no scruple in saying, in the presence of
our friends here, that I am a man who has, for some years, con-
tended against the pressure of pecuniary difficulties." The next day
David receives a distressing epistle from Mrs. Micawber (not a
request for money; as David himself acknowledges later on, Micawber never approaches him for money). Perplexed by this awkward intelligence, David thinks it correct to visit Micawber. Half-
way to the hotel, he notices the coach with "Mr. and Mrs. Micawber
up behind." "As they did not see me," David "thought it best, all
things considered, not to see them"; and "with a great weight taken
off my mind" he turns away, "relieved that they were gone" (ch.
17). The moral slyness that taints David's "relief" betokens a darkness darker than Kincaid suspects or admits.

Almost without exception, criticism of *David Copperfield* has
ignored the social and moral implications of David's response to
the problems of the Micawber family, implications that are heightened by Traddles' contrasting response. In chapter 28 David, quite
smitten by Dora, invites Traddles and the Micawbers for dinner
at his chambers. Mrs. Micawber—with her rather admirable "I
never *will* desert you, Micawber!"—launches into a consideration
of the relative merits or demerits of a variety of possible professions for Mr. Micawber. David's response is the silent laughter
of superior derision. In this entire business of the Micawbers,
David, curiously, is never willing to admit the *reality* of their condition, or the reality of his bonds with them. He either seeks to
obliterate those bonds or, in better times, adopts the stance of a
genteel outsider. David sees Mrs. Micawber as "the sort of woman
who might have been a Roman matron, and done all manner of
heroic things, in times of public trouble." It is important to realize
that this judgment may well be the judgment of the reader; however, coming as it does from David, to whom the Micawbers have
given succor, the distance implied in David's amused observation
smacks of callousness, a callousness that is evident in all subsequent contexts in which David is faced with the Micawbers. Now
Micawber slips a letter into David's hand and detains Traddles for
a moment at the top of the stairs. David, suddenly alerted, cor-
ners Traddles to warn him, "If I were you, I wouldn't lend him

anything." Traddles smiles and says that he hasn't "got anything to lend." David points out that he has "got a name" to lend. Traddles, shocked, returns, "You call *that* something to lend?" It is impossible to ignore, I think, the contrasted perspectives of value presented here. We also remember that Traddles owes nothing to the Micawbers; David does. Traddles has, of course, already helped Micawber with a note, which cost him £23,4s,9½d.

The theme is renewed in chapter 34. Traddles tells David that Micawber has been obliged to change his name to Mortimer "in consequence of his temporary embarrassments." It is significant that, whereas David has given Micawber up for lost, Traddles should see Micawber's difficulties as "temporary." Traddles then discloses to David that, David's counsel notwithstanding, "Mrs. Micawber was in such a dreadful state that I really couldn't resist giving my name to that second bill we spoke of here. You may imagine how delightful it was to my feelings . . . to see the matter settled with it, and Mrs. Micawber recover her spirits." The human assumptions that inform the David-Micawber-Traddles context are those of Henry Fielding, whom Dickens approved of enough to name one of his sons after. They are the assumptions that Fielding took from the Latitudinarian preachers of his day. The ethical polarities of their value system are defined by spontaneity or unmotivated goodness, on the one hand, and prudent calculation, on the other. In this sense, contrary to Needham's position, not David but Traddles might be seen as Tom Jones or Parson Adams, and David as a potential Blifil—fully realized later in Charlie Hexam.[25] Traddles asks that David spare Peggotty to help him purchase back his own old furniture. David condescends but on "condition . . . that he should make a solemn resolution to grant no more loans of his name, or anything else to Mr. Micawber." Against David's prudent suspicion of Micawber, Traddles voices his confidence: "He don't tell me that it *is* provided for, but he says it *will* be. Now, I think there is something very fair and honest about that!"

When Micawber, the second bill also having fallen, hands his IOU to Traddles, and Traddles accepts it gladly, this is David's ugly reflection: "slippery as Mr. Micawber was, I was probably indebted to some compassionate recollection he retained of me as his boy-lodger, for never having been asked by him for money" (ch. 36).

That David retains no such reciprocal recollection of Micawber's tenderness to him strong enough to make him want to assist Micawber is, of course, the irony.

In chapter 39 David tells us that a shadow has fallen between him and Micawber: "I clearly perceived that there was something interprosed between him and me, since he had come into his new functions." The "new functions" relate to Micawber's employment with Heep. As Micawber begins to discover Heep's wrongdoing, he becomes more and more "reserved" from Mrs. Micawber. Mrs. Micawber writes to David that to her "this is heartbreaking." David, barely reading the letter, recommends that "she should try to reclaim Mr. Micawber" (ch. 42). Sometime later, Micawber himself writes to David, "*not* [on] an object of a pecuniary nature," but about Heep, the "devil." After Micawber exposes Heep, David, who has thus far kept the Micawbers out of his mind and out of his affairs as much as he can, is now "thankful for the miseries of my younger days which had brought me to the knowledge of Mr. Micawber." The context, however, makes David's thankfulness dubious: it relates more to the elimination of Uriah Heep, less to the "knowledge" of Micawber (ch. 52). In contrast, Traddles' praise of Micawber is refreshingly free of any ambiguity: "I must do Mr. Micawber the justice to say . . . that although he would appear not to have worked to any good account for himself, he is a most untiring man when he works for other people." And again: "I must, once more, give Mr. Micawber high praise. But for his having been so patient and persevering . . . we never could have hoped to do anything worth speaking of. And I think we ought to consider that Mr. Micawber did right, for right's sake, when we reflect what terms he might have made with Uriah Heep . . . for his silence" (ch. 54). It is amazing, when one thinks of it, how little David actually does "for other people."[26]

The David-Micawber context has one other aspect, eloquent in its irony. The Micawbers, everyone recognizes, are drawn closely after John and Elizabeth Dickens. Now the Micawbers have a son who, at the time the family leaves for Canterbury to take up employment with Wickfield and Heep (comparable with the Dickens' move from Chatham to London?), is "twelve or thirteen" years of age — that is, the age of young Charles Dickens at the time of the Warren's blacking-factory episode. Traddles and David visit

the Micawbers (the Mortimers); David notes with detached supe-
riority the "limited . . . resources" of "this lodging"—a turn-up
bedstead and a "wash-stand jug" in which the Micawbers make
their "Brew." What about the "twelve or thirteen"-year-old boy
caught up in this "limited" environment? David-Dickens shows no
recognition of the reflexive applicability of the circumstance. His
pontifical comment on "Master Micawber" is that the "promising"
young boy was "very subject to that restlessness of limb which
is not an unfrequent phenomenon in youths of his age" (ch. 36).
The only other time David notices this young boy he remarks:
"Master Micawber, whose disposition appeared to have been
soured by early disappointment, and whose aspect had become
morose, yielded to his better feelings, and blubbered" (ch. 52).
David betrays none of that sympathy for Micawber's son which
we know he and Dickens angrily demanded in a like situation.
The self-absorbed failure of imagination that defines this aspect
of the David-Micawber context amounts to a collapse of the moral
intelligence. This seems clearly not just David's failure but Dickens' as well. If David's reference to Master Micawber's "promising" nature and to his "early disappointments" suggests that Dickens
sees the irony, then the withdrawal of recognition and empathy
from Micawber's son is, indeed, a grave indictment of the narrator. The problem is that there is no countering authorial voice
in the context to indicate that such is the case. As with Steerforth,
Dickens' undifferentiated ambivalence towards David remains morally and artistically disquieting. For instance, how much of the
contrast between David's and Traddles' treatment of Micawber does
Dickens clearly see? How much of David's treatment of Traddles
does he not endorse? The texture of the narrative voice suggests
that Dickens seeks to submerge these contexts. Yet, the narrative
is there, and the new narrative form gives us a chance. The problem, however, acquires a deeper significance in the context of
David's relation to Uriah Heep.

VI

I think it is fair to say that the quality of critical comment on
Uriah Heep has only recently begun to reflect the intensity of

David's and Dickens' engagement with him. Often the comment has not extended beyond the obvious: Heep is "repellent"; he is a "skillful and vindictive schemer" who is rightly "brought to defeat."[27] Lucas states that "Dickens hates Uriah Heep and so does David,"[28] but does not tell us why. Cockshut sees him as a "puzzling and unsatisfactory character," although he notes, suggestively, that Heep's "repellent physical nature is unfairly overstressed."[29] Barbara Hardy suggests that "the relationship between the two men seems to reveal more than is ever made explicit, and the study of David's loathing for Uriah is one of the most powerful insights in the novel."[30] This promising generalization remains unexplored.

Leonard F. Manheim was the first critic of the novel I know of who saw Uriah Heep's function as being that of a surrogate. Manheim, however, neutralizes that insight by positing that David and Heep are opposites.[31] David and Heep are not opposites but essentially varying formulations of an identical drive. I think that we begin to be close to the structural center of the narrative if we see Steerforth and Heep together in relation to David, illuminated by David's projections onto them. David's adoration of Steerforth and loathing of Heep go together; so does David's emphasis on Steerforth's physical charm and on Heep's physical ugliness. David refuses to judge Steerforth because he conflates what he regards as his own noble impulses with Steerforth's image (impulses which are class impulses). Parallel to this conflation, David loathes Heep because he sees the worst possibilities of his own actuality realized in Uriah Heep. The intermeshing details of the David-Heep context bear this out.

Some of these details are so obvious as to be actually striking when they are noticed. David and Heep are both fatherless (as is Steerforth). David mentions his father three times without ever placing him socially with any explicitness, an omission that lends weight to Cockshut's observation about David's ambiguous class position. The only dubious evidence of David's gentility, then, is the house at Suffolk. Now, Uriah Heep's father was a sexton, an officer of the church, in charge of the sacristy and, later on, of the entire church property, with a residence of his own. There is therefore only a thin line between David and Heep in the matter of background, a significant fact that tends to be muffled in the narrative. This, of course, is not at all David's view of the matter; in fact, much of his attitude toward Heep is conditioned by his view of Heep as socially inferior. David and Heep are both articled clerks, working for the law. David and Heep alike seek the daughter of the man each works for, Dora Spenlow and Agnes Wickfield. David has a great aunt whom he calls "my second mother" (ch. 23) and who is good to him. Heep has a mother who, Agnes tells us, is full of "praises of her son" (ch. 35). Just as David desires to be distinguished, to climb the "ladder" of success," so does Heep. David projects himself as a "gentleman," although his claims are questionable at the least; correspondingly, Heep capitalizes on humbleness without being humble. At the time that Micawber "astonishes" Heep, Uriah, with his customary insight into David (which, as I pointed out, David acknowledges), points sharply to the ironies of their respective stances: "You think it justifiable, do you, Copperfield, you who pride yourself so much on your honour and all the rest of it, to sneak about my place, eavesdropping with my clerk? If it had been *me*, I shouldn't have wondered; for I don't make myself out a gentleman (though I never was in the streets either, as you were . . .), but being *you*!" Uriah's parenthetical shaft is snide but true. Whereas it is first the Micawbers and then Betsy Trotwood who keep David off the streets, Heep sustains himself and his mother (to whom he is, Agnes tells David, "a very good son" [ch. 35]) through work—work which becomes a central Carlylean value of David's life as he cuts his way through a "forest of difficulty" (ch. 37).

At the time of their first considerable encounter, David finds Heep intently "going through Tidd's *Practice*." David supposes that Uriah is "quite a great lawyer," but Uriah protests that he is only a "very umble person." "Then, when your articled time is over," David persists, "you'll be a regular lawyer." "With the blessing of Providence," returns Heep. David then prognosticates that "perhaps you'll be a partner in Mr. Wickfield's business, one of these days . . . and it will be Wickfield and Heep, or Heep late Wickfield" (ch. 16). When David visits the Heep household, he offers to teach Uriah Latin. Heep comments that "there are people enough to tread upon me in my lowly state, without my doing outrage to their feelings by possessing learning. . . . A person like myself had better not aspire." David's response is, "I think you are wrong, Uriah" (ch. 17). The texture of this colloquy is strange and psychologically arresting. There is a wishful inwardness to everything David says here to Uriah, a reflexive empathy: David might be talking aloud of himself, of his own repressions and desired objectives. A long time after this, of course, Uriah will remind David that David was "the first to kindle the sparks of ambition in my umble breast," indeed proving himself a "prophet" ("Don't you remember saying to me once, that perhaps I should be a partner in Mr. Wickfield's business, and perhaps it might be Wickfield and Heep?" [ch. 25]), and David will hate him for it, without, it is crucial to note, any hint yet of Heep's misappropriations. What is it that evokes David's loathing? The fact that he finds Heep where he himself should like to be, successful and close to Agnes?

Understandably, the more David hates Uriah the more he emphasizes Heep's physical ugliness. When Heep tells David, "Oh, Master Copperfield, with what a pure affection do I love the ground my Agnes walks on!" David has the "delirious idea of seizing the red-hot poker out of the fire, and running him through with it" (ch. 25). David may aspire to Dora, but for some curious reason Heep may not aspire to Agnes, although, as Heep points out, he has "as good a right to [such an aspiration] as another man" (ch. 39). The fact is that Heep's physical appearance is necessary for David to distinguish himself from Heep: it, in a sense, becomes the only condition of class. Steerforth may violate Emily, but Heep may not even think of Agnes. It is interesting that Agnes herself never shows the kind of loathing and dread of Heep that David does. Even Micawber, the instrument of Heep's downfall, is willing to give Uriah his due so long as Heep's misdeeds are unknown to him. When David questions Micawber as to how he has been treated by Heep, Micawber answers: "My friend Heep has responded to appeals to which I need not more particularly refer, in a manner calculated to redound equally to the honour of his head, and of his heart." This is more than we have seen David do for his friend Micawber. There can be no question that Micawber is speaking with objectivity; when David says, "I should not have supposed him to be very free with his money," Micawber states that "I speak of . . . Heep as I have experience" (ch. 39).

Further experience is precisely what causes Micawber to denounce Heep.

Heep's repelling appearance and the schemes through which he gains ascendancy — reflecting Dickens' view now of the social consequences to which an unbridled individualism can lead — are too much against him for us to save him. Nevertheless, the details of Heep's life as well as of his ambition are also those of David's life and ambition. Heep tells David of the "foundation school" where he was sent as a boy: "They taught us all a deal of umbleness — not much else that I know of, from morning to night. We was to be umble to this person, and umble to that; and to pull off our caps here, and to make bows there; and always to know our place, and abase ourselves before our betters. And we had such a lot of betters!" David comments: "I fully comprehended now . . . what a base, unrelenting, and revengeful spirit, must have been engendered by this early and this long, suppression" (ch. 39). The story of Heep's life is what the story of David's life might have been had there been no Betsy Trotwood. When Betsy Trotwood says of Heep, "He's a monster of meanness!" Traddles points out, "Many people can be very mean, when they give their minds to it" (ch. 54). This is, indeed, a very disquieting reflection, challenging gentility with Dostoevskian insight.

With Uriah Heep, then, Dickens achieves an all-important reversal: where Dick, Smike, Nell, and Paul are rewarded in Oliver, Nicholas, Kit Nubbles and Walter Gay, David is *punished* in Heep.[32] Dickens, even while he continues to be nostalgic and protective, has now the strength to include in *David Copperfield* a dramatization of the debasement attendant upon a pursuit of the goal that capitalism has set for the ambitious individual; and Dickens projects this debasement at two graded levels. Where the individual seeking success is cushioned somewhat by birth and timely aid, individualism may yet retain the facade of gentility even while it is seen, inevitably, to jettison human claims. For David, the Peggottys, the Micawbers, even Traddles, are deadwood that must, at bottom, be shed when the time comes; and in any case, superior coachmen, chambermaids, and butlers must be granted prior regard — not to speak of Steerforth. "Scholastic record," "economic progress," "short-hand," and so forth must be protected and shored up, rendered invulnerable to romantic exigency and moral claim. Dickens, the author, aids here and there: he gets rid of obstacles that lie along the "ladder," to wit, Dora. It is Needham's view of Mrs. Copperfield and Dora that "Dickens sympathetically allows them to die young—perhaps the kindest fate life can provide for them and theirs." Needham, in effect, shames Dickens' own generosity. Another way Dickens, the author, helps is by rewarding people who have suffered David's unjust neglect with arbitrary plums—Micawber, Peggotty, Traddles —so that his guilt is assuaged and perhaps even forgotten altogether.

Where the individual lacks attendant advantages, however, the bourgeois dream takes on a starker character. In an important sense, Heep's career, especially his defense of it, is the strongest indictment of the conundrum in which capitalism places the individual who would freely appropriate into his own career the system's iniquitous social theory of expropriation: if he has not sufficient clout, he becomes the criminal. Not that Dickens' view here entirely coincides with my statement of what we *can* take away from the novel. When David receives news of Barkis's death, Steerforth observes that "people die every minute, and we mustn't be scared by the common lot." He goes on to advise: "No! Ride on! Rough-shod if need be, smooth-shod if that will do, but ride on! Ride on over all obstacles, and win the race!" (ch. 28). This is precisely the advice Heep puts into practice. Yet David loves the one and loathes the other. With the Steerforth-David-Heep concatenations, however, Dickens is well-placed for the devastating critique that the fiction of the fifties is to provide. Heep acquires the status of a new thesis, and the spirit of Heep is given full range and reign in *Bleak House, Little Dorrit,* and *Hard Times.*

CHAPTER 7

The Novels of the Fifties:
A Connecting Note

In *Dombey and Son* Carker, the scheming subordinate, and Walter Gay, the residual antithesis to Paul, remain morally polarized in the Ralph Nickleby–Nicholas pattern. Dickens' great leap in *David Copperfield* consists in showing, through the coalescing of Heep and David, that Carker represented, not an individual case, but a historical tendency. The manager-manipulator finally has something to say to the genteel aspirant after success. One might say that in Heep Carker's melodramatized teeth acquire real bite. Dickens thus brings himself to a point where he can render the spirit informing Carker and David/Heep as a ubiquitous reality: in *Bleak House* one fog clouds everybody in London, and not a soul is exempt from the curse of the Chancery; nobody can "get out of the [Chancery] suit on any terms, for we are made parties to it, and must be parties to it whether we like it or not" (ch. 8).[1] In chapter 47 of *Dombey and Son* Dickens had spoken of Dombeyism as a disease potent enough "to blight the innocent and spread contagion among the pure." That passing metaphor acquires the status of an all-pervasive cultural epidemic in Tom-All-

Alone's revenge (ch. 46). The image of Lady Dedlock dead on the steps of a pauper's burial ground dressed as a brickmaker's wife has the collapsing historical force of the image of the dead Agamemnon in Yeats's "Leda and the Swan." The worlds of Dombey and of Mrs. Brown are here brought together not as plot but as cause and effect. In *Little Dorrit*, the residual formalism and pretense of the Dombey-Edith connection is shorn naked and deconstructed in the Merdles' marriage. Merdle says to Mrs. Merdle: "You supply manner, and I supply money" (bk. 1, ch. 33). Mrs. Merdle, in turn, makes a powerfully denuding statement on the status of marriage within the social world of mid-Victorian capitalism: "As to marriage on the part of a man, my dear, Society requires that he should retrieve his fortunes by marriage. Society requires that he should gain by marriage. Society requires that he should found a handsome establishment by marriage. Society does not see, otherwise, what he has to do with marriage" (ibid.). We recall that Mr. Merdle has chosen Mrs. Merdle primarily as a jewel stand, a privately symbolic version of England's "great exhibition." The larger point to make about Mrs. Merdle's summation is that if marriage is a metaphor for relatedness, then the terms of her statement go to define, inclusively, all relations under capitalism, especially in its highly speculative phase. Only gain, the new reason stipulates, ought to connect individuals. The whole novel is, of course, an enactment of that principle — something that lends justice to George Bernard Shaw's well-known remark.

In *Bleak House* John Jarndyce provides Richard Carstone a Carlylean piece of advice (also à la Samuel Smiles): "Trust in nothing but in Providence and your own efforts" (ch. 13). After Heep, however, the further crass extreme of this benign philosophy — its properly *lumpen* extension — is voiced eloquently by Rigaud to Clennam: "I sell anything that commands a price. How do your lawyers live, your politicians, your intriguers, your men of the Exchange? How do you live? How do you come here? Have you sold no friend?" And, finally, "Society sells itself and sells me: and I sell Society" (bk. 2, ch. 28). "Bargain and sale," "hiring and letting" — Dombey's phrases come to full life and all-pervading realization in *Little Dorrit*. The myth embodied in Jarndyce's statement about self-help — the myth, that is, of equal opportunity

under a system that enshrines inequality—is taken up for withering exposure in *Hard Times*: "This, again, was among the fictions
of Coketown. Any capitalist there, who had made sixty thousand
pounds out of sixpence, always professed to wonder why the sixty
thousand nearest Hands didn't each make sixty thousand pounds
out of sixpence, and more or less reproached them every one for
not accomplishing the little feat. What I did you can do. Why don't
you go and do it?" (bk. 2, ch. 1). Given the hypocrisy embodied
in that advice, Dickens also, appropriately, expresses now a wholly
different attitude towards education. The old emphasis on good
schooling—and therefore the old animus against bad schools and
bad teachers (Squeers, Mrs. Pipchin, Blimber's academy)—receives
a perceptive, though ironic, closure in Smallweed's succinct statement in *Bleak House*: "We have never been readers in our family.
It don't pay" (ch. 21). (*Hard Times* is to be Dickens' most decisive
statement on the subject.) After *David Copperfield* generally, education comes to mean something wholly different to Dickens from
the business about going to school, acquiring a good "scholastic
record," and launching into a career. In *Great Expectations*, the
least literate man is to be the most educated. And Gaffer Hexam
in *Our Mutual Friend* will simply declare: "I can't read, nor I don't
want to" (bk. 1, ch. 3).

In *Bleak House* and *Little Dorrit* Dickens' quite "modern" purpose is also to dramatize the paradox of the lonely urban crowd.
Thus the connecting metaphors themselves—Chancery, Circumlocution Office, Prison, and so forth—reveal the absence of human connectedness. Everywhere, Dickens anticipates the crowds
crossing London Bridge in Eliot's "The Waste Land," eyes fixed on
the next man's heel. So that the isolated image of the autonomously
mechanical, mindless, monster train of *Dombey and Son* translates now into a universe of mechanistic individuals and institutions. For example, in *Little Dorrit*, we are told that the Circumlocution Office, a terrifying, Kafkaesque reality, "went on
mechanically everyday." Pancks—carrying forward the enactment
of the consciously self-divided individual from Morfin in *Dombey and Son*, Inspector Bucket in *Bleak House* ("duty is duty and
friendship is friendship," he says to Rouncewell), and leading on
to Jarvis Lorry in *A Tale of Two Cities* and Wemmick in *Great*

Expectations[2] — Pancks is in part "a little labouring steam engine." Rugg is a "professional machine"; Mrs. General's manners are a "piece of machinery"; and in Mrs. Clennam's house "morning, noon, and night, morning, noon, and night, each [recurs] with its accompanying monotony, always the same reluctant return of the same sequences of machinery, like a dragging piece of clock-work" (bk. 1, ch. 28). The apotheosis of this stasis, its putrid rottenness, will be conveyed in the image of Miss Havisham, for whom all time will stop as correlative to thwarted self-interest.

This general consistency of advance is reflected equally in Dickens' endings. After the marriage of Walter Gay and Florence, and the union between David and Agnes, Esther's marriage to Woodcourt has relatively less force; at least, having been witness to the drama of the novel, it strikes us as a mere act of faith. Its content is, in any case, deromanticized in the marriage of Arthur Clennam and Amy Dorrit, which communicates itself only as a sad and sober partnership between two quite exhausted people. And, if we may anticipate, despite Bulwer-Lytton and the so-called changed ending of *Great Expectations*, the novel makes it clear that there is no marriage between Pip and Estella, so that Dickens complies with the sure knowledge that his compliance makes no real difference to his sure demonstration.[3] With *Our Mutual Friend* Dickens' ending acquires a purely fictive character: the Wrayburn–Lizzie Hexam match is self-consciously offered as utopia.

Another progression may be traced: the new Bleak House of Esther and Woodcourt is dismantled in the crash of the Clennam house. In *Great Expectations*, home is quite literally lost; and in the last novel, as I suggested, home is a wished-for hereafter. Nor is it at all inappropriate that consequent upon this pattern of a totalized crisis, of fall everywhere, the next novel — the last of the fifties — should be one that enacts a historical explosion. *A Tale Of Two Cities* escalates, within this pattern, Krook's combustion into an all-engulfing revolution — a climax that expresses the need for a new beginning. Sydney Carton's wishful projections bear directly on the scene at home: "I see a beautiful city and a brilliant people rising from this abyss, and, in their struggles to be truly free, in their triumphs and defeats, through long years to come, I see the evil of this time and of the previous time of which this is the natural birth, gradually making expiation for itself and wearing out" (bk. 3, ch. 15).

Bleak House, Hard Times, and *Little Dorrit,* then, explore as a *Zeitgeist* the mid-Victorian crisis of value. The insights gained in the writing of *David Copperfield* enable Dickens to present a harrowing critique. The fog over London, the Chancery teeming with predatory lawyers and lawyers' clerks, the epidemic of poor Jo, Gradgrind's principles, Bounderby's Dombey, the Circumlocution Office, Bleeding Heary Yard, the Tite Barnacles, the Merdles, the Casbys, the Pancks — all these, and much more, constitute a relentlessly extended exploration of the social and economic drives of an entire culture that have been forcing their reality on Dickens' art in his bitter battle with himself. Yet, one may ask, where now in these novels is the place of the self-image? Esther, Amy, Arthur, are all vindicated. The general contagion of the rendered experience of these novels hardly threatens the equanimity of their virtue. The contradictions that made David interesting with respect to Dickens' ongoing evaluations are shelved. As Dickens portrays the mid-Victorian crisis of value, he seems simultaneously obliged to posit the adult self-image as a repository of value. It is a peculiarly new and interesting *Aufhebung.* The stasis of the Oliver-Dickens stage was such as to render Dickens' art in half measure correspondingly mechanistic. Overcoming that stasis enables Dickens to produce the fiction that he does up to *A Tale of Two Cities;* and yet as he dramatizes in the fifties not stasis but the dynamics of an all-encompassing social order, of a world falling to pieces, he finds himself, in an adult capacity, much like the Waverley hero, immobilized into watching this new dissolution from the distance of a felt pathos. The suffering of Esther, Amy, and Arthur, although it confirms their virtue, does not *generate* value. In this crucial sense these are novels of vision — a vision, no doubt, made possible by Dickens' whole struggle from the thirties — not of discovery. In *Great Expectations,* the new synthesis will be the most complete yet because in that novel Dickens will take himself *through* the full life-experience of these antecedent novels, making the dynamics of lived suffering a precondition of the forging of the human value that Esther, Amy, and Arthur merely posit. If *Bleak House* and *Little Dorrit* take away from Oliver and David their successes, enriching such character types in turn with sympathy, *Great Expectations* will go a step beyond and involve and implicate them fully in the taint of the general life that Dickens has now rendered with engagement and without weakness. The form of *Great Expectations* is its very experience because the form of Pip's life issues from Pip's effort to approach his suffering with a generative intelligence. As Pip suffers, as he becomes sensitized to others' suffering, he reflects; and as he reflects, his life moves forward, carrying with it the shape of the whole novel. What Esther, Amy, and Arthur simply sustain, Pip must discover. The distance from David to Pip involves the shock of a multiple recognition. Thus David's story must be retold. A quick look at the framing imperatives of David's and Pip's lives suggests the quality of the retelling: David had to be taken out of the warehouse; Pip will seek to go back to the forge. Where David's frantic need to put Mealy Potatoes behind him has Dickens' blessing, Dickens *cannot* — in the face of the transparent, realized integrity of the new novel — quite manage for Pip the return to the forge.

CHAPTER 8

Great Expectations:
Being as Relatedness

I

David, we know, was very much on Dickens' mind as he sat down to write *Great Expectations*. He wrote to Forster that the new "book will be written in the first person throughout, and . . . you will find the hero to be a boy-child, like David." Further, "to be quite sure I had fallen into no unconscious repetitions, I read *David Copperfield* again the other day."[1] Dickens' comment about avoiding "repetitions" is most instructive, considering that nearly all the major configurations of character and situation in *David Copperfield* reappear in *Great Expectations*. For instance, Pip, "like David" is the hero; Traddles returns as Herbert Pocket, Steerforth as Drummle, Betsy Trotwood as Miss Havisham, Agnes as Biddy, Wickfield and Spenlow together as Jaggers, Micawber as Joe, and Micawber's Australia as Magwitch's Australia. Yet none of these are repetitions, and Dickens knows what he is about. Traddles now receives recognition in Herbert Pocket; Steerforth is demystified in Drummle; Micawber is elevated in Joe (and lost); Agnes is rendered in Biddy (and also lost); Betsy Trotwood, the man-hater, degenerates into Miss Havisham; the Wickfield and Spenlow figures are sharply amalgamated in Jaggers to make a finer point about a new, nonhuman "professionalism"; and Micawber's Edenic Australia translates into a place of banishment for Magwitch. Taken together, these momentous revisions and reversals carry Dickens to a new *Aufhebung*: in a single work he dramatizes the creatively assimilated tensions of the entire antecedent oeuvre. In Pip's account the piecemeal past, personal and historical, becomes conscious and intelligible and, thereby, whole.

In a delightful piece of writing on the novel, Christopher Ricks says most truly that the greatest things about *Great Expectations* are also the most obvious.[2] The simplicities of this novel are, however, arrived at after — and *through* — many complex confrontations, and our whole view of the quality of Dickens' achievement must improve considerably when we keep in mind everything that has preceded *Great Expectations*. For instance, the infallible hold Dickens now has on the speaking voice — perhaps the single most significant determinant of the novel's success, its "To Autumn" cadence — is unthinkable without Dickens' experiments with David and Esther. In Pip's voice Dickens brings together the combined rhythms of David's and Heep's consciousness. The adult, storytelling Pip who reflects and comments upon the action of the narrative functions as the new antithesis to his own image as that image unfolds — clearly in a way that David's voice does not. And the complexity of Pip's experience of the world and his experience of himself achieves emotional credibility in the credibility of that antithetical voice. Dickens' control of the art now is a consequence and an expression of a serenely distanced life experience, felt deeply even as it is distanced; its telling carries only the necessary and fulfilling pain of self-knowledge. With Pip, Dickens at least is a wide-eyed witness to himself and, simultaneously, to a whole culture.[3] Even the contradictions that remain are now fully sentient.

II

The first thing to realize about *Great Expectations*, I think, is that it is not a novel about money in the sense in which the three previous novels might be said to be about money. The power of money in *Great Expectations* does not overtly define the explorations of its action. This is not to say that the explorations of the novel can be meaningfully understood without our awareness that the power of money is constantly the controlling background of its experience. But it is a background, and Dickens is not concerned now with repeating the demonstrations of the three previous novels; rather, he suggests in more subtly existential terms the implications for the self of the pressure of a prevailing culture. That pressure is now gathered — as the *déjà donné* — in the figure of Compeyson, who embodies the sum of Dickens' explorations in the three previous novels and, as such, effectually dictates the destinies of most of the principal characters as a preestablished cause. The story of Pip is the achieving of an authentic self.[4] It is a discovery, simultaneously, of the illusory nature of the sanctioned definitions of freedom and bondage and an effort to give to these concepts a more authentic meaning.

When Pip is being set up in new clothes by Mr. Trabb, he notices that Mr. Trabb's attitude toward Trabb's boy has become abrasive and insensitive; Pip comments that "my first decided experience of the stupendous power of money, was, that it had morally laid upon his back, Trabb's boy" (ch. 19). It is the sort of comment that testifies overtly to the crassness to which people and relationships descend under the inducement of gain and is, altogether, of a rather obvious nature (after *Bleak House* and *Little Dorrit*). Coming as the statement does at the end of the first part of the book (immediately before Pip's remove to London), even its irony is, perhaps, rather obvious: it is not Trabb's boy but Pip who is soon to be "morally laid upon his back." In *Great Expectations* Dickens' more rewarding focus is not to be on these external demonstrations of the power of money but on the destructive internal alchemies that the power of money can generate. Likewise, Dickens' engagement with morality is to extend further: Dickens, I think, is now concerned with the ways in which morality ultimately becomes a definition of the condition of man's self. Our criticism of *Great Expectations*, then, ought to move from the many exhaustive analyses of the obviously moral nature of Pip's degeneration towards an isolation of how Dickens seeks to connect that process with the meaning of Pip's selfhood and his discovery of relationship. Pip's new clothes, for instance, might furnish a more important insight about Pip's existence and essence than his comment about Trabb's boy.

Pip's naming of himself recaptures that significance of anonymity and nonbeing that attached to the caprice of Bumble's naming of Oliver. "Pip," however, means "seed," and that analogy from nature establishes nicely the generative metaphor of growth and enlargement. But in Pip's germinal condition, the genus as well as the species of the plant-to-be are not merely precarious but confused. Who is Pip? What is Pip to be, other than, that is, a "bundle of shivers" or the residue of dead names on dead gravestones? Pip is something that Mrs. Joe "fish[es] . . . up by the hair" or uses as a "connubial missile" (ch. 2) to throw at Joe, thereby turning him into a projectile of her loveless nonbeing. To Pumblechook, Pip is merely an "extra-boy to frighten birds" (ch. 7), until, of course, Pip's promised elevation seems to put a value on Pip. What Pip's narrative of the events before his meeting with Estella (ch. 8) establishes is that only through Joe does Pip find a locus for self-definition. Only Joe, a "larger species of a child," can Pip treat as "my equal" (ch. 2), because only Joe is cognizant of Pip as a being independent of Pip's function or his possibilities. Mrs. Joe's identity derives from her "government" of the household and from her sense that she controls the possessions of the household, such as they are. Joe's selfhood, on the other hand, is independent of possession. When Pip is struggling with his child's conscience prior to his "larceny," he makes the curious comment that "I never thought I was going to rob Joe, for I never thought of any of the housekeeping property as his" (ch. 2). And in his response to Magwitch a little later, Joe validates Pip's insight: "God knows you're welcome to it [the food Pip has stolen] — so far as it was ever mine" (ch. 5). Mrs. Joe's "cleanliness," which is "more uncomfortable and unacceptable than dirt itself," is the expression of a dis-ease rooted in self-hatred and self-rejection, as is her "trenchant way of cutting . . . bread-and-butter," a veritable Mass of hatred (ch. 2). Contrarily, Joe's essence is a nonalienated essence, a condition of self-recognition and self-trust. Interestingly, Joe is also sought to be presented as a nonalienated worker controlling his own means of production, the forge, which is projected in the novel not as an exploitive structure but as an extension of Joe's fulfilling creativity. Joe, one notices, forges a family, as opposed to Jaggers, who separates mother and child. Surrounded by Joe's self-trust, Pip is able to find for himself "a local habitation and a name." Joe, "a fair man" and "a good judge" (ch. 5), and Pip are "fellow-sufferers" in the face of Mrs. Joe's tyranny. Indeed, Joe's strength of selfhood and the compassion emanating from it allow him to wish that he "could take it all on" himself (ch. 7).

In chapter 7 (the chapter immediately preceding Pip's introduction at Satis House) Joe tells Pip about his own past. The story Joe tells is that of a father who, in the quality of his concern for the young Joe and his mother, counterpoints Mrs. Joe. Joe is quite sensible of having been deprived of a formal education because of his father's drunkenness but remembers with sympathy that "my father were that good in his hart that he couldn't abear to be without us." Joe, "rendering unto all their doo, and maintaining equal justice betwixt man and man," insists that his "father were that good in his hart, don't you see?" Of course, Pip "didn't see"; nor can the reader until one realizes that the point of Joe's comment is not necessarily an objective one but a phenomenological point about intersubjectivity: other people have only the value that one grants oneself. Value, that is, is not a function of countable paraphernalia but of conviction; and conviction in the other can result only from conviction in the self. Joe is convinced that, "whatever the world's opinions" Mrs. Joe is "a fine-figure-of-a-woman," give or take a "little redness, or a little matter of Bone here, or there, what does it signify to Me?" What does "signify" is that the individual can find purposive identity only through empathy. So, Pip and his sister are valuable enough for Joe to gather into a family. And as the self is fulfilled only through relation, relation must correspondingly be sustained at some expense of self:

"And last of all, Pip—and this I want to say very serious to you, old chap—I see so much in my poor mother, of a woman drudging and slaving and breaking her honest hart . . . that I'm dead afeerd of going wrong in the way of not doing what's right by a woman, and I'd fur rather of the two go wrong the t'other way, and be a little ill-conwenienced myself. I wish it was only me that got put out, Pip; I wish there warn't no Tickler for you, old chap; I wish I could take it all on myself; but this is the up-and-down-and-straight on it, Pip, and I hope you'll overlook shortcomings."

This is indeed the "up-and-down-and-straight on it"; and this is also what it means to "come to a J and a O," so that "'Here, at last, is a J-O, Joe.'"[5] Joe reads himself in a more fundamental sense than the alphabetical. His name acquires the weight and meaning of a hieroglyphic, an emblematic language of compact metaphor rather than of plain representation, and Joe's self is coterminous with the corporeality of *J* and *O*. Joe's scholarship (as opposed to Pip's or Jaggers') is of a kind that allows the perception of true value, enabling him to make "my own self" the epitaph for his father: "Whatsume'er the failings on his part, Remember reader he were that good in his hart." The making of the epitaph is to Joe like "striking out a horseshoe complete, in a single blow"; Joe forges value as he forges horseshoes.[6] The intensity of the heat that goes to mold and weld metal in the forge, then, becomes comparable to the intense stress of conscious experience that alone can mold and weld human life. And when Pip admits that he "dated a new admiration of Joe from that night," and "had a new sensation of feeling conscious that [he] was looking up to Joe in [his] heart," he suggests his first felt recognition of the true nature of value: to *be* is to be *human*, and to be human is to be strongly defined in creative relatedness.

III

The *Gestalt* of Pip's first visit to Satis House recalls that of Cathy Earnshaw's visit to Thrushcross Grange. In Edgar Linton, Cathy encounters her first gentleman, superior to the dirty-nailed Heathcliff. In Estella, Pip senses the power of poise that similarly derives from grooming and from the solid security of property. In contrast to Estella, Biddy "was common, and could not be like Estella" (ch. 17). In each case, class functions as the determinant of consciousness. When Cathy returns to Wuthering Heights, she notices for the first time that Heathcliff is "so dirty";[7] only "if you wash your face and brush your hair, it will be all right." Heathcliff's response is, of course, that "I shall not stand to be laughed at. I shall not bear it" (*WH*, 63). As Arnold Kettle points out in his excellent essay on the novel, Cathy's preference for Edgar Linton is a social preference, a capitulation to the bourgeois dream, made tormenting by Cathy's existential certainty about its wrongness ("I *am* Heathcliff," she tells Nelly [*WH*, 91–97]).[8] Subsequently, when Heathcliff turns to Nelly and says, "Nelly, make me decent," wishing he had "light hair and a fair skin" (*WH*, 65, 66), he is not spurred by any bourgeois lure but by his all-consuming need to recover Cathy. Heathcliff's return as a sophisticated gentleman (attendant with irony) and his ruthless expropriation of the Earnshaw and Linton properties do not denote his conversion to bourgeois values but constitute, as he tells Nelly, "a *moral* teething"—a getting back at the bourgeois world that has deprived him of his life's meaning by way of its own mechanics of property. Not for a moment does Heathcliff see himself fulfilled through that mechanics; instead of causing self-rejection in Heathcliff, the Linton world brings about catastrophic self-assertion. Heathcliff's sense of value remains undaunted, and his resultant moral anger makes a bonfire of lives that he sees as valueless. Cathy Earnshaw has time enough to repent. However, while she is dying, she accuses Heathcliff of having made her suffer; Heathcliff points out to her with unrelenting allegiance to the truth of his vision of the meaning of their relationship that it is not he who has betrayed her: Cathy's has been, existentially, a fatal self-betrayal. In marrying Linton, Cathy has alienated herself from the deepest convictions of her own being, an alienation for which there is neither cure nor forgiveness: "*Why* did you betray your own heart, Cathy? I have not one word of comfort. You deserve this. You have killed yourself . . . I have not broken your heart—*you* have broken it" (*WH*, 189).

Great Expectations has none of the intensity of presentation that Emily Brontë's extraordinary novel has. Nevertheless, the quality of experience that defines Cathy Earnshaw's betrayal of herself also illuminates the nature of Pip's self-betrayal. Satis House causes in Pip a more total self-rejection than Thrushcross Grange does in Cathy. When Estella designates Pip a "common labouring-boy" (ch. 8), she makes Pip conscious of a self that is not, but in Estella's scale, *ought* to be his; and where Heathcliff responds to the

Lintons with the full force of his authentic self, battling and defeating the effete world of bourgeois propertyism, Pip caves in to it because he accepts its valuation of himself. Pip is, indeed, reified into the wax that defines Satis House, and as brittle wax, Pip fragments under the force of Estella's "contempt": "Her contempt for me was so strong, that it became infectious, and I caught it" (ch. 8). The burden of Joe's dialogue with Pip in chapter 7 was to underscore the strength of selfhood deriving from a felt perception of human value, "whatever the world's opinion"; Estella affects Pip through estrangement. Estranged from himself, Pip is suddenly troubled by things that "had never troubled me before"—his "coarse hands and . . . common boots" (ch. 8). Throughout Pip's prolonged repentance it is not his betrayal of Joe *per se* that torments him, except in the sense that he sees that betrayal simultaneously as self-betrayal: "All other swindlers upon earth are nothing to the self-swindlers, and with such pretences did I cheat myself" (ch. 28). Pip here already begins to recognize the justice of what Miss Havisham says to him, cruelly and dishonestly, a long time afterward: "You made your own snares" (ch. 44).

Twice Estella, candle in hand like a ritual goddess, leads Pip (petrified into obedience) through dark passages (chs. 8, 11), and the dark passages become correlatives of the deepening anarchy of Pip's nonbeing. Each time "the rush of the daylight quite confound[s]" him. Estella's cruel admonition to Pip "not [to] try to brew beer there now" because "it would turn out sour" (ch. 8) is charged with an irony that informs the further movement of Pip's self-rejection: in trying to "brew" a new identity for himself, Pip does "turn out sour" because Pip's endeavor, unlike Joe's forging of horseshoes, is impelled not by a creative self-trust but by a self-defeating alienation. When Pip returns from Satis House, he is stricken by "a dread of not being understood" because he no longer understands himself. Consequently, says Pip, "I think of myself with amazement [estrangement] when I recall the lies I told." The self-told lies, of course, already suggest with irony the fragility of Pip's great expectations. It is only in Joe's presence that Pip has the courage of self to confess; and Joe's comment, in its axiomatic simplicity, is directed at restoring for Pip the equilibrium of his valuations: "lies is lies," and lying is no "way to get out of being common" (ch. 9). Joe's moral sense is a projection of his happy self-knowledge — a self-knowledge embodied in his human interactions. Pip must ponder things for a long time indeed before he can translate his painful self-knowledge into felt initiatives of selfhood.

As the time comes for Pip to leave Miss Havisham's service, Joe is summoned to Satis House. Pip is not only "ashamed" of Joe but distressed that Joe will not show gratitude to Miss Havisham for inquiring whether he did not expect any "premium with the boy." (The situation is repeated in chapter 18 as Jaggers asks Joe a similar question, a situation that elaborates in sharply polarized terms the two prevailing views of value in the novel. To this I shall return.) Irked — that is, morally irked — by Pip's surprising insistence that he answer Miss Havisham, Joe says to Pip: "That were not a question requiring an answer betwixt yourself and me, and which you know the answer to be full well No. You know it to be No, Pip, and wherefore should I say it?"[9] The sad irony, of course, is that Pip is no longer sure enough of himself to be able to reciprocate Joe's certitude. Joe's response to Pip here, as to Jaggers later on, contains Dickens' central human insight in *Great Expectations*. Joe is consistently the only character in the novel who voices a nonexploitive view of human relationships. He sets no "premium" on Pip's labor, refusing to see Pip as an investment, refusing to reify Pip's human potential into commodity.[10] What is important, Joe says, is that "you and me do our duty, both on us by one and another" (ch. 13); clearly, in speaking of "duty" Joe seeks to establish a categorical imperative that he perceives as being true to the deepest morality of man's self.

In chapter 18 Jaggers brings tidings of Pip's "great expectations." Jaggers asks what Joe will have for agreeing to cancel Pip's indentures. Joe answers, "Lord forbid that I should want anything for not standing in Pip's way." Jaggers, the powerful advocate of "professionalism" ("I am paid for my services, or I shouldn't render them"), thinks Joe's sentiment "pious, but not to the purpose." The point is, Jaggers persists, "Do you want anything?" Joe's answer is the same as his answer to Miss Havisham, "No." When Jaggers admonishes Joe in the best legal way to "recollect the admission you have made" and not to "try to go from it presently," he is merely expressing his habitual value-system, dictated, as in Joe's case, by the quality of *his* particular self-knowledge: services are not rendered unless they are paid for. Joe is infuriated by the suggestion: "Who's a-going to try?" Undeterred in his correctness, Jaggers mentions "compensation"; Joe asks, "Compensation what for?" and is told, "For the loss of [Pip's] services." Thereupon, "Joe laid his hand upon my shoulder with the touch of a woman. I have often thought [of] him since . . . in his combination of strength with gentleness. 'Pip is that hearty welcome,' said Joe, 'to go free with his services, to honour and fortune, as no words can tell him. But if you think as Money can make compensation to me for the loss of the little child—what come to the forge—and ever the best of friends!—'" Jaggers, convinced that Joe is a "village idiot," insists that Joe candidly state his terms, cancelling with his anaesthetized amorality the possibility of any human communication with Joe. Joe, "suddenly working round him with every demonstration of a fell pugilistic purpose," invites Jaggers to "come on" "if you're a man": "Which I meantersay that what I say, I meantersay and stand or fall by." Having coolly followed correct procedure, Jaggers advises Pip to call at his office in London, but on the explicit understanding "that I express no opinion, one way or another, on the trust I undertake. I am paid for undertaking it, and I do so." Pip wishes to be a gentleman; Jaggers will do a good job for good money; Joe is the only one who is willing to "stand or fall" by the truth of himself, being "a man." Joe is his own best evidence, and it is of no account how he may or may not look to a rich lawyer from the city of London.

Pip, with his painful recognition of the value that resides in Joe, opts against "myself" when he leaves the forge in order that he may be "good enough" for Estella: "Dissatisfied with my fortune, of course I could not be; but it is possible that I may have been, without quite knowing it, dissatisfied with myself" (ch. 18). So he tells Biddy, "I want to be a gentleman." At the same time Pip also has the interesting thought that "if I could only get myself to fall in love with [Biddy]" "*that* would be the thing for me," since Pip believes that he "should have been good enough for" Biddy. Biddy retorts with a rather withering irony, "Yes, I am not over-particular." In this new context David and Agnes come of age. By the time that Pip recognizes that he may never be "good enough" for Biddy and returns to make a plea, Biddy is wedded to the only man who is truly "good enough" for her (ch. 17).

As apprentice to Joe, Pip is "dejected" from the very "first working day." The "only thing I *am* glad to know of myself in that connection," Pip tells us, is that he "never breathed a murmur to Joe." Nonetheless, during this time he feels the "influence" of Joe and knows his "self" strangely "touched" by Joe's presence: "I know . . . that any good that intermixed itself with my apprenticeship came of . . . contented Joe, and not of restlessly aspiring discontented me." Pip remains "faithful" because "Joe was faithful." Yet, as Estella's face rises in Pip's mind, "I was haunted by the fear that she . . . would exult over me and despise me" (ch. 14). The more ill at ease he feels at her thought, the more Pip desires to approximate himself to Estella — Estella, who is, ironically but feasibly, the most totally alienated of all the characters in *Great Expectations*. As time passes, Pip will have a clearer perception of the fact that Estella has no self: "You speak of yourself as if you were some one else" (ch. 33).

For the time being, however, as Joe agrees to cancel Pip's indentures, Pip "felt that I was free." He speaks of his "emancipation" and promises himself to pour "a gallon of condescension upon everybody in the village." Since Pip sees freedom as a release from commitment, thoughts of Magwitch assail him (Dickens' insight being unfaltering), and Pip hopes that Magwitch "had doubtless been transported a long way off, and that he was dead to me, and might be veritably dead into the bargain." Pip directs Biddy to tend to Joe's "learning and his manners" in order to prepare for his removal into a "higher sphere" when "I fully come into my property." Biddy replies that Joe "may be too proud to let any one take him out of a place that he is competent to fill, and fills well and with respect"; in what Biddy says here, she not only conveys a sure knowledge of herself but also reiterates the central statement of the novel: one is happy only when one is happily oneself. (On the rather disquieting social implications of Biddy's statement I shall comment in my concluding chapter.) The truth of Biddy's observation is suggested immediately, when Pip dresses up in his new suit of clothes; Pip feels as much "at a personal disadvantage," as unlike himself, as Joe "in his Sunday suit." Nevertheless, very ill at ease, Pip sets out for "London and greatness" (ch. 19).

IV

In chapter 20 the novel moves to the second part of Pip's great expectations. The forge gives way to London, and Jaggers replaces Joe as the presiding father figure. Struck and "scared by the immensity of London" Pip sees "Little Britain" (appropriately Jaggers' establishment) as "ugly, crooked, narrow, and dirty." Jaggers' room is "a most dismal place" lighted by a "skylight only" and spiritually defined by the "two dreadful casts on a shelf"—symbols of an order of progress and well-being based on human liquidation. While Pip is standing by, lost, he witnesses Jaggers' clerk shove "this gentleman out with as little ceremony as I ever saw used"; the only "ceremony" that is observed in "Little Britain" is the ceremony of cash. As Jaggers is accosted by several terrified clients, his unvarying refrain is, "Have you paid Wemmick?" The business of justice, Pip notices, is conducted through bought witnesses:

"Well, Mas'r Jaggers," returned Mike, in the voice of a sufferer from a constitutional cold; "'arter a deal o' trouble, I've found one, sir, as might do."
"What is he prepared to swear?"
"Well, Mas'r Jaggers," said Mike, wiping his nose on his fur cap this time; "in a general way, anythink."

Finally, when Jaggers directs Pip to Barnard's Inn, he is certain that Pip will "go wrong somehow, but that's no fault of mine" (ch. 20). Unlike the forge, London is not the world of human commitment; it is a world where the only operative commitment is to "number one," and Jaggers is now merely an installed and lawful Fagin. As Pip wonders about "which side was . . . [Jaggers] on?" he answers, "Money." Being "professional, only professional," Jaggers is a "man-trap" (ch. 24) who leaves the doors and windows of his house tantalizingly open.

Chapters 20 through 40 of *Great Expectations* contain Dickens' French novel. In Jaggers' world Pip is to discover that his "emancipation" is, in essence, anarchy, his sense of being "free" after leaving the forge transforming subtly into his growing awareness of being totally unfree. What is left of Pip's being is thus exhausted into a nothingness.

I suggested earlier that in chapter 9 Pip's "lies" about Satis House function as the first parody of Pip's expectations, of their fantastic and illusory nature. In chapter 22 Herbert Pocket fantasizes about grand "Capitalism," with the difference that his fantasy is rendered with a self-conscious sense of absurdity. Herbert Pocket's account, in effect, becomes a parody of the methodologies of laissez-faire individualism: "Then the time comes . . . when you see your opening. And you go in, and you swoop upon it and you make your capital, and then there you are! When you have once made your capital, you have nothing to do but employ it." "Then there you are!" Pip does not know quite where. He can see that Herbert, "having already made his fortune in his own mind," is to be commended for not being "puffed up." But as Pip tries to correlate Herbert's account with what he *sees* of London, he is stricken with thoughts of "the poor old kitchen at home", and London falls "hollow on [his] heart." Pip, of course, does not realize that it is not *Herbert's* fortune alone that is made "in his own mind" but Pip's as well. Yet, the newly seen context subtly turns Pip's concentration away from fortune and upon his own felt condition. In relation to *David Copperfield* this constitutes a subtle but significant reversal of focus and interest: the movement of the *Bildungsroman* in the earlier novel is one of steady consolidation; that of Pip's life in London is defined by a scattering dissociation, a critical deconstruction that in one book now assembles the deconstruction of the whole oeuvre, such as threatens to splinter Pip's very identity. Pip's splintered consciousness of self is suggested powerfully in chapter 45 as Pip, "wide-awake" at night, stares at the "foolish Argus" light which is "perforated with round holes."

After Pip has "established [himself] . . . and had gone backwards and forwards . . . several times," he is given the intelligence that he "was not designed for any profession." Pip's education is to consist solely in "'hold[ing] my own' with . . . young men in prosperous circumstances" (ch. 24) — to wit, the "Finches of the

Grove." When Pip first thought of his elevation, we recall, he fantasized about "what I would buy if I were a gentleman" (ch. 15); in London Pip discovers that *buying* indeed becomes his only objective definition as a "gentleman": "I soon contracted expensive habits, and began to spend an amount of money that within a few short months I should have thought almost fabulous" (ch. 25). When Pip, Herbert, and Drummle visit Jaggers' house, Pip, amazed at himself, "found that I was expressing my tendency to lavish expenditure . . . and to boast of my great prospects, before I quite knew that I had opened my lips" (ch. 26). The play of Pip's consciousness here, as during much of his discovery of himself, is revealing: it is a moment in which Pip, unsure of who he is, literally catches himself turning into Veneering in response to and under the influence of an intimidating social context. Pip is terrified of Joe's visit to London because he has not the courage, the preparedness, to be reminded of himself. His condition is summed up nicely by Joe when he remarks that Barnard's Inn is not quite fit for a "pig." And Pip's alienation is complete when Joe calls him "sir." Altogether, Pip is seen as a respectable pig. The only place other than Barnard's Inn that Joe visits in London is the "Blacking Ware'us" (ch. 27): not only is this the best tribute Dickens can pay Mealy Potatoes but, simultaneously, a rather telling rebuke to Barnard's Inn. Dickens can, finally, bring himself to be harsh on himself.

Christopher Ricks points out that one of the principal reasons that we feel with Pip is that he is constantly unhappy.[11] The more Pip pursues his new life (a life without an informing center) the more unfree he becomes, and the more unfree he is the more unhappy he becomes. His dream of Estella for which he sought to be free of Joe turns into a wretched bondage: "I knew to my sorrow, often and often, if not always, that I loved her against reason, against promise, against peace, against hope, against happiness" (ch. 29). Caught in the web of "ill-regulated aspirations," Pip is swallowed by an "indefinite and unsatisfactory" illusion (ch. 30). When Estella arrives in London, she details to Pip the instructions she has been given; Estella's verbs are inexorably imperative ("I am to"; "you are to"; "we are to") — verbs that eloquently testify to the bonded lives of Pip and Estella: "We have no choice, you and I, but to obey our instructions. We are not free to follow our own devices, you and I" (ch. 33). Soon, Pip realizes sadly that Estella "speak[s] of . . . [herself] as if [she] were some one else" (ch. 33). "Free" of Joe, Pip has no idea where his money comes from or to what end he lives. The more money he obtains the more debts he incurs. "Late hours and late company" characterize Pip's wasteland-life: "There was a gay fiction among us that we were constantly enjoying ourselves, and a skeleton truth that we never did." And Dickens offers a finely tested insight into the crowning illusion of this life of illusions: knowing, inevitably, that they are "getting on badly," Pip and Herbert settle down to that old trick of juggling figures. Pip and Herbert stare ugly facts "out of countenance" (ch. 34). They make allowance, they leave "margins," they try every sleight of financial gimmickry, but they always come up short. No pen-and-ink wizardry can quite repair the bankruptcy of value in Pip's life.

At this nadir of despair Magwitch (repeatedly referred to as "my convict") returns as Pip's third father figure. This defines for Pip a graduated fall from Joe and the forge to Jaggers and London to Magwitch and the underworld. With horror, Pip awakens to "the truth of my position" (ch. 39); and the "truth" is, as Estella had pointed out to Pip, that Pip has been as free as a "puppet" (ch. 33) —a "brought-up London gentleman" (ch. 39) over whom his "owner" gloats with "admiring proprietorship" (ch. 40). Pip has, indeed, been a commodity. Where David was thrilled to discover that Steerforth still saw him as "my property," Pip is desolate at his discovery; not Brownlow but Magwitch is now the patronizing benefactor.

The second movement of the novel ends with the disintegration of Pip's self: "I thought how miserable I was, but hardly knew why or how long I had been so, or on what day of the week I made the reflection, or even *who I was that made it*" (ch. 40; emphasis added). Pip suggests that catastrophic nature of his discovery through an elaborate anticipatory parable (an "Eastern story") in chapter 38:

In the Eastern story, the heavy slab that was to fall on the bed of state in the flush of conquest was slowly wrought out of the quarry, the tunnel for the rope to hold it in its place was slowly carried through the leagues of rock, the slab was slowly raised and fitted in the roof, the rope was rove to it and slowly taken through the miles of hollow to the great iron ring. All being made ready with much labour, and the hour come, the sultan was aroused in the dead of night, and the sharpened axe that was to sever the rope from the great iron ring was put into his hand, and he struck with it, and the rope parted and rushed away, and the ceiling fell. So, in my case; all the work, near and afar, that tended to the end had been accomplished, and in an instant the blow was struck, and the roof of my stronghold dropped upon me.

Having identified himself with visions of real estate (Estella in her soulless condition being a part of that real estate), Pip sees his identity come crashing down as the "ceiling fell." For five days Pip suffers the torment of recognition and of an adjustment of conciousness, a suffering that Dickens is able to render with a finely controlled and felt inwardness. And consistent with the conceptual commitment of Dickens' novel, the worst of Pip's anguish is caused, most ironically, by his realization that Magwitch "is attached to me, strongly attached to me. Was there ever such a fate!" (ch. 41).

V

The third and last movement of Pip's consciousness defines the new *Aufhebung*. Having been brought to the abyss of a negative recognition through a self-absorbed consciousness, Pip in time achieves a positive view of that recognition. What Pip has to comprehend is that Magwitch's reentrance into his life is quite the best "fate" that could overtake him. Appropriately, this realization begins with the knowledge that Magwitch's fate has been in all generative essentials identical to his own. Magwitch has "no more notion where [he] was born than [Pip has] — if so much." The naming of Abel Magwitch is revealed to have been as arbitrary (in its nonsignificance) as Pip's own: "I know'd my name to be Magwitch, chrisen'd Abel. How did I know it? Much as I know'd the birds' names in the hedges to be chaffinch, sparrer, thrush." As a child Magwitch has known the rejection that Pip has, having "grow'd up took up" as Pip was "brought up by hand": "So fur as I could find, there warn't a soul that see young Abel Magwitch . . . but wot . . . either drove him off, or took him up." Whereas Magwitch has covered up Pip's "larceny," giving him his chance to remain respectable, there was no such protection for Magwitch when he was "athieving turnips for my living." And young Magwitch, "a ragged little creetur" (Pip, we recall, remembers himself as "a bundle of shivers"), thus "got the name of being hardened" (ch. 42).

Magwitch's relationship with Compeyson is charged with implications that release the central ironies of the book. Magwitch is taken in by Compeyson because Compeyson "set up fur a gentleman . . . and he'd been to a public boarding-school and had learning. He was a smooth one to talk, and was a dab at the ways of gentle folks"—quite the apotheosis of Heep. Also, Compeyson sports "a watch and a chain and a ring and a breast-pin and a handsome suit of clothes." Armed with this front, "Compeyson's business was the swindling, hand-writing forging, stolen bank-note passing, and such-like. All sorts of traps as Compeyson could set with his head, and keep his own legs out of and get the profits from and let another man in for, was Compeyson's business" (ch. 42). In Compeyson, then, Dickens gathers every characteristic practice upon which he saw the speculative world of mid-Victorian financial skulduggery based. And yet, Magwitch, Compeyson's worst victim, seeks essentially to produce in Pip another Compeyson, assuming that to be a successful "gentleman" is to be a Compeyson. That legality in this context treads a precariously thin line is suggested by the morally odious legality of Jaggers. Between Magwitch and Compeyson the latter always has the advantage because, as for "character," was it not "Compeyson as had been to the school, and warn't it his school fellows as was in this position and in that, and warn't it him as had been know'd by witnesses in such clubs and societies [a Finch of the Grove]" (ch. 47)? Inevitably, Pip's further evaluation of himself and of Magwitch must be made in the light of the reflexive emotional and moral force of Magwitch's account—in the light, that is, of Magwitch's "fate." However mistaken and ironic Magwitch's perceptions are in relation to the making of Pip, his commitment is a response to an essentially human situation: Pip has brought him food and freedom. Simultaneously, Magwitch's childhood relates not only to that of Pip but, significantly, also to that of Joe, who not only survives his father but is able—as Magwitch is with respect to Pip—to offer a commitment to him, as he does to Pip. It is thus conceptually consistent that Magwitch, when he reappears, should increasingly reorient Pip's consciousness towards Joe. Pip can recover himself now only by actively engaging in self-fulfilling commitment, as Joe and Magwitch have done. Immediately, Pip's first such act is to secure from Miss Havisham nine hundred pounds for setting up Herbert Pocket—"the only good thing I had done" (ch. 52). And *doing* an other-directed "good thing" in turn frees Pip for his recovery of himself.

Pip's "one dominant anxiety" (ch. 47) begins to be the safety of Magwitch. When Magwitch is removed (as Mr. Campbell) to the waterside home of Herbert's fiancée, Pip remarks that "I little supposed my heart could ever be as heavy and anxious at parting from him as it was now" (ch. 46). Pip seeks honestly to understand Magwitch not as Magwitch is seen and placed by society but in terms of the motivating commitments of Magwitch's being. As the escape is under way Pip notes that Magwitch "was the least anxious of any of us." "If you knowed, dear boy," Magwitch tells Pip, "what it is to sit here alonger my dear boy and have my smoke . . . you'd envy me." Pip responds that he thinks he understands now what "freedom" is: he wonders with a new sense of meaningful paradox that "for any mastering idea, . . . [Magwitch] should have endangered his freedom and even his life." Pip also understands that "perhaps freedom without danger" (the "danger," that is, of a "mastering idea") may not, after all, be worthwhile. After Magwitch is retaken, and Compeyson is dead (suggesting Pip's release from the bondage of the bourgeois dream), Pip "took . . . [his] place by Magwitch's side" and "felt that that was . . . [his] place henceforth while he lived." Pip's "repugnance" for Magwitch melts away because he is able to see that Magwitch has been "a much better man than I had been to Joe." Writing of the last hours of Fagin's life, Hillis Miller speaks of Fagin's attempt, while in the cell, to befriend Oliver, to establish a bond with him, and of the "profound consubstantiality" of the two as Oliver walks a few steps towards the gallows with Fagin.[12] That gesture achieves its lived apotheosis now in the consubstantiality, the willed union, between

Pip and Magwitch—that is, between an Oliver made deeply conscious in history and a redeemed Fagin. It is an apotheosis that encapsulates the totality of Dickens' development.

I suggested earlier that Magwitch helps reorient Pip's consciousness toward Joe; Pip now voices for himself (as a statement of achieved self-knowledge) the categorical imperative that Joe had stated to him a long time ago. "May you and me do our duty," Joe had said; Pip says to Magwitch, "I will be as true to you as you have been to me" (ch. 54). As the time for Magwitch's trial draws near, Pip's selflessness generates for him a self-fulfilling "meaning": "I grew to understand [Magwitch's] meaning very well" (ch. 56)—a "meaning" that is contained in the slightest pressure of an infirm hand. And climaxing the existential rationale of this entire movement is Pip's charged hallucination: every face now "settle[s] down into the likeness of Joe. . . . Whoever came about me, still settled down into Joe" (ch. 57). Indeed, Pip is able to see that "Here, at last, is a . . . Joe" (ch. 7).

In this reading of *Great Expectations* I have emphasized the rediscovery of human value *in* human relatedness, superseding the pulls of legacy, property, and personal career. This structure of meaning involves the redefining of many acquired cultural terms—such as education, success, crime, guilt, repayment, and, finally, value—and the jettisoning of "normative" social goals. In what Dickens discards, or overcomes, we have the sense of great achievement; yet, in what he puts in place of what has been rejected there may well be room for discomfort, and my reading can invite the charge that it encourages the metaphysical. This for the reason that the positive values which Dickens offers seems to lie outside—or, at least, to be independent of—historical necessity; and they are placed in a subjective-imaginative framework, although emerging, as I have tried to show, from a sustained enactment of bourgeois Victorian reality. For instance, Dickens' view of Joe may tend to enshrine or mythologize naïveté and mere illiteracy, to perpetuate the myth of the self-serene worker of the Ruskinesque utopia, or to valorize individual relationships disproportionately. There are two things to be said. One is that in presenting Joe—and the novel, with ample quotation—I see myself as presenting what *Dickens* represents in *Great Expectations*; the other is that in the face of the felt weight of the experience of the novel (and, indeed, of the whole process up to *Great Expectations*), of its realized status as conviction, it seems churlish to undervalue what Dickens has been through and what he has put behind in preference to what might be the doctrinal innocence of his new thesis. It is hardly a mean achievement that in the face of his own atomistic compulsions and of an alienated and alienating social reality, portrayed in *Great Expectations* with a total mastery of the deeply historical, Dickens should with the demonstrated sincerity of confession reenshrine the social value of *free* human interaction, and reestablish nonexploitive relatedness as the essence of what it means to be human.[13]

VI

In speaking of the ending(s) of *Great Expectations*, Martin Meisel holds that "in the total architecture of the novel neither ending is very important. Each gives a similar peaceful account to a more or less completed structure."[14] Insofar as this concerns the final ending with the two versions, I think Meisel's view is sound; the novel does make it immaterial whether Pip and Estella part or do not part. Even in marriage there can be no closure to their lives, but rather, only fresh self-discovery and initiatives into a much larger connectedness than matrimony encompasses. For Meisel, however, the book ends with Pip's return from Cairo and his finding of himself anew in little Pip, suggestive of a new beginning. The implications of Pip's sudden removal to Cairo and of his eleven long years of profitable commerce there do not enter into Meisel's consideration. Nor does he notice the awkward haste of Pip's removal or the awkwardness of Dickens' writing about it. Milton Milhauser, on the other hand, isolates — quite soundly, I think — three distinct endings in the novel, following upon each other in a hurried, linear, and structurally dysfunctional manner.[15] He sees the first and to him the most satisfying ending in chapter 58 with Pip's return to the forge after his illness, the second with Pip in Cairo, and the third with Pip back in London, "settling romantic accounts with Estella" (that is, the ending with two versions). Milhauser argues that Pip leaves the forge not because of Biddy's marriage but because, "for class or cultural reasons, he cannot stay." Also, "Joe is a better man than Pip, but, by a different set of values, Pip has become a better man than Joe — and Dickens measured by both scales." Therefore, Milhauser points out, whereas Pip's return to the forge was morally imperative, it was practically impossible.

Milhauser's brief but acute article still offers, in my view, the best analysis of the problem of the ending in *Great Expectations*. With Milhauser's analysis I find myself in close agreement. However, I differ with him insofar as he draws a totally unsympathetic reading from his own analysis. I rather think that Milhauser's perception about the first two endings might be reversed to support an argument that would seem to suggest the strength of a new candor in Dickens' attempted resolution of the old problem.

When Pip returned to the forge, his "purpose was, that [he] would go to Biddy" and plead that he is "a little worthier of you than [he] was — not much, but a little" (ch. 57). Pip finds Biddy married to Joe and understands that there is no longer a place for him at the forge. It is rather crucial that we see the weight that the loss of Biddy carries for Pip at this stage (Milhauser disregards this entirely). The fact that Dickens can (after David and Agnes) countenance this loss as well as countenance its alienating consequence for Pip evidences, I think, a major advance. Pip's deepest "need" after all that has happened is "of a hushing voice and a soothing hand" (ch. 57). In the new circumstance, the *adult* Pip's further stay at the forge must seem inconceivable, not only on his own account but for the happiness of Joe and Biddy. His decision to remove himself from the forge, then, is more than a mere ploy; it is a painful act of self-exile. When Pip leaves, he tells Joe and Biddy that he "shall never rest until I have worked for the money with which you have kept me out of prison." At the same time, Pip is aware that "if I could repay it a thousand times over, I [do not] suppose I could cancel a farthing of the debt I owe you, or that I would do so if I could" (ch. 58). Curiously, then, Pip's removal from home to Cairo defines a movement parallel to Magwitch's banishment in Australia. Magwitch applied himself to making all the money he could to establish the child who had been kind to him. There is, however, a crucial difference — a difference that takes in all the weight of the experience of the novel: first, Pip's is a self-imposed banishment, and second, with all that is behind him, Pip cannot believe that what he owes Joe can ever be repaid in money.

Milhauser quite rightly points out that despite Pip's moral growth his experience has nonetheless made him a gentleman of sorts — listening to Handel (as opposed to Joe's "Old Clem") and acquiring a "taste for reading." But that recognition, painfully enough, constitutes for Dickens the strength of a new and ironic admission: Pip *can* use what he has picked up socially in London's wasteland to find himself a career. And the irony of that admission extends to Dickens himself; in 1861 Dickens *is* rich, a fact that he simply cannot wish away. And yet, what an agony of consciousness (the whole of *Great Expectations*) is now offered as amelioration. Whereas Dickens can in no way alter the social fact (he cannot altogether go back to Warren's Warehouse, as Pip cannot to the forge), in itself suggestive of Dickens' acknowledgment of the force of history, the quality of his consciousness about the fact as well as the quality of the rendered art in *Great Expectations* illuminates the contradictions of the social problematic with a depth and rigor of perception that constitute more than an apology. Dickens brings an entire age to confession.[16] One needs, of course, to keep the dialectic of the entire canon in mind to appreciate the magnitude and the significance of the movement from Oliver to Pip. Whatever Dickens has previously cloaked with compromise he now recognizes and dramatizes as contradiction. For that contradiction Dickens has, admittedly, no cure, but at last he does not spare himself the pain of confession.

CHAPTER 9

Our Mutual Friend:
A Concluding Note

I do not propose to offer any detailed analysis of the enacted experience of *Our Mutual Friend*. Its river, its drowning, its sham drownings, its resurrections, its London and its dust heaps, its Veneer and Podsnappery, its system of shares, have received extended as well as acute attention. I propose to comment only on three matters: Dickens' further movement from Pip vis-à-vis the dialectic of the self-image, the limits of the dialectic in Dickens, and the question Dickens leaves himself and the reader at the end of his last completed novel.

Carrying forward his concern with the forging of value, Dickens offers in book 3, chapter 5, of *Our Mutual Friend* an explicitly Marxist critique of the high-Victorian view of value. Admittedly, Dickens does not follow the theoretical projections of the Marxian analysis of history, but as seen and enacted insight — commodity economy, conspicuous consumption, exploitation and alienation, deriving from what Bella calls "misprized riches" (4.13)[1] — Dickens' diagnoses here are wholly those of Marx and Engels.[2] Rokesmith, the secretary, urges Boffin, the Golden Dustman, to "fix my salary." Boffin, bringing Rokesmith in line with the terms of capitalism, points out that what the secretary means is not "salary" but "wages." Boffin further admonishes that a poor man ought not to be proud, because "being poor, [he] has nothing to be proud of." As "a man of property" Boffin explains: "A sheep is worth so much in the market, and I ought to give it and no more. A secretary is worth so much in the market, and I ought to give it and no more." As a capitalist employer he is, however, willing to stretch "a point or two," since under the capitalist transactional system there may be allowed some room for bargaining. Having determined the secretary's "worth" to be two hundred pounds a year, the Golden Dustman stipulates that "If I pay for a sheep, I buy it out and out. Similarly, if I pay for a secretary, I buy *him* out and out." The secretary therefore understands that his employer "purchase[s] my whole time." The framing determinants of value, then, are supply and demand and the "market-price" of commodities, human labor being only one of the commodities. (We recall the terms of Polly Toodle's hire at the Dombey house.) This contrived and syncopated situation between Rokesmith and Boffin finds its real, extended presentation in the Podsnap-Veneering-Fledgeby world — a world where "traffic in Shares is the one thing to . . . do" (1.10) and where starvation is faulted for being "not in good taste" (1.11). In this world Dombey and Bounderby are finally the only ruling deities, who, in denying their subservient workingmen their identities (Rokesmith is equated with the "time" and the "worth" of his labor), deny them their existential freedom.

In wishing, then, to "climb" the "scale of society" (4.2), Charley Hexam seeks to be Podsnap, for the Podsnaps define the "scale of society."[3] And this scale includes Charley's teacher, Bradley Headstone, as well. Headstone, whose fragmented mind is a "warehouse" full of fragmented "stock" (2.1), places himself, ultimately, not by his "learning" but by his "station" (2.15), the learning having been merely the *modus operandi*. Headstone points out to his promising student that by passing "a creditable examination," "you will be one of us."[4] Charley, therefore, desires urgently "to forget the bills upon the walls at home" so that he can "get up in the world." When he visits Lizzie at Jenny Wren's, Charley cannot understand what his sister can "have to do with" Jenny; resentful of being "pull[ed] . . . back" (2.1) by Lizzie because of her "ridiculous fancy of giving herself up to another" (2.15), Charley desires his sister "to settle . . . in some Christian sort of place" (2.1). It is, of course, very revealing that "a Christian sort of place" is seen by the culture as a materially decent sort of place, a position entirely consistent with Mr. Podsnap's Malthusian resentment against the poor and with his conviction about his own *election* — a conviction based upon his wonderful success. (Bulstrode in *Middlemarch* is to be the complete presentation here.) The situation between Charley and Lizzie Hexam, then, is closely analogous to that between Pip and Joe. Charley wants to "carry" Lizzie "up with me," but Lizzie is "very well where I am"; Lizzie "want[s] for nothing." Charley would like to give the river a "wide berth," but Lizzie "can't get away from it" (2.1).

As Charley plays Pandar for Headstone, he is entirely convinced that Lizzie could have no conceivable grounds for turning his teacher down, not only because Headstone is so "respectable" but also because Lizzie surely must see that Charley's best interests would be nicely served by such a match: ergo, "Respectability, an excellent connexion for me, common sense, everything!" Surely, Lizzie cannot fail to recognize that "my way is yours" (2.15). As in *Great Expectations*, the social coercion is simultaneously an existential coercion. Lizzie's refusal is therefore utterly incomprehensible and infuriating to her brother: "Do you know that he is worth fifty of you?" (2.15). "Worth" is for Charley, no doubt, informed by the "scale of society." (The opposite definition of value is early expressed by Jenny Wren: "You're more to be relied upon than silver and gold," she says to Lizzie [2.7], setting her up as the touchstone by which the world of the dust heaps is to be judged.) "Upon my soul," says Charley, "you are a pretty piece of disinterestedness! And so all my endeavours to cancel the past and to raise myself in the world, and to raise you with me, are to be beaten down by *your* low whims." Never once false to the philosophy of "number one," Charley is determined that Lizzie "shall not disgrace" him, for "after I have climbed up out of the mire, you shall not pull me down . . . I *will* have nothing to do with you for the future" (2.15).

Charley's climbing, of course, stretches across every claim of commitment to relationship. In time he is to "drop" his "best friend" (2.15), Headstone, considering himself as having been compromised through the attempt on Eugene's life and congratulating himself for the "deliverance," "no thanks to you" (4.7). The most selfish of climbers, he accuses Headstone (who has, with proper irony, taught Charley everything he knows) of having been "so selfish, and so concentrated upon yourself, that you have not bestowed one proper thought on me" (4.7). What makes Headstone tragic is precisely the fact that he knows this well enough, as well as he knows that he is lost because he has "no resources in myself . . . no confidence in myself . . . no government of myself" (2.15). Charley Hexam's bitterness is generated by his vengeful perception that "every effort I make towards perfect respectability, is impeded by somebody else through no fault of mine." Regardless of such impediments, Charley sees his "prospects" as being "good" and "mean[s] to follow them alone" (4.7). With Headstone, Podsnap, the Veneerings, the Lammles, and Fledgeby available to us, Dickens need not belabor where Charley's "prospects" may lead. Whatever tentative possibilities of "return" to Joe's forge Dickens might suggest for Pip, for Charley there is no return to Lizzie's analogous fireside. As Dickens' vision of the British bourgeoisie becomes a vision of total darkness, his treatment of the self-seeking self-image hardens, at long last, into total rejection: Charley spoke, Dickens tells us, "as if there were no softening old time behind him. Not wonderful, for there *was* none in his hollow empty heart. What is there but self, for selfishness to see behind it?" (4.7). From Oliver to Charley Hexam Dickens travels a long road indeed.

Dickens dramatizes two contrasted modes of education in *Our Mutual Friend*, the formal and the experiential. The formal mode involves the passing of creditable examinations and defines the lives of Bradley Headstone and Charley Hexam (Boffin, we know, remains — or is meant to remain — unimpaired by Mr. Wegg's erudition);[5] the experiential mode applies to Bella Wilfer, assimilates the structure of discovery from *Great Expectations*, and explores similarly the implications for the self of a world ruled by the "Gospel according to Podsnap."[6] In the chapter "In Which an Innocent Elopement Occurs" (a chapter equal to the best in Balzac

or Flaubert, those dramatists *par excellence* of the bourgeois dream)
Bella — Dickens' first and only French woman, as irresistible as
she is delightedly aware of her wickedness, Mammon's willing
worshipper — overwhelms her equally delightful lover-father with
the rush of her mercenary fantasies: "I have made up my mind
that I must have money, Pa . . . and . . . I have resolved that I
must marry it" (2.8).[7] Bella's fantasy (which takes up the entire
chapter) is a veritable *tour de force* and confirms all of John Harmon's existential anxieties. The woman that old Harmon has de-
creed his son must marry is a woman who has, on her part, "resolved" to "marry" money ("it"). John Harmon must therefore
determine *who* Bella is — as opposed, for example, to Lizzie Hexam,
of whom her brother acknowledges, sadly without any illumina-
tion for himself, "What she is, she is, and shows herself to be" (2.1).
John Harmon — Dickens' Duke of Vienna or his Prospero — then
sets up a testing context: since money (that is, dust) is what Bella
would have, she will be given enough exposure to it so as to know
its truest taste. The Golden Dustman will be her guardian angel.
The situation, one notices, is informed with an irony similar to
that which attends the Duke's abdication of government to Angelo in Shakespeare's *Measure for Measure,* an abdication made
on the supposition that of all people in Vienna Angelo is the one
incorruptible man. Angelo, we know, surprises himself greatly.
In Boffin's case, similarly, the contrivance and the play stretch to
a point where he begins to be threatened in reality and, indeed,
cannot wait to disengage himself from the role he has been as-
signed. That Dickens can show this possibility saves the Boffin
context, I think, from being mere contrivance.

The Boffin experiment completes for Dickens his exploration
into the Brownlow figure — that is to say, its full deconstruction.
Beginning with a good man whose goodness is beyond question,
he ends with a good man who even in a fictive experiment tends
in reality to disintegrate through exposure to money. So that Dickens, making now the best use of art, provides at once both the
ideal and the real.[8]

Additionally, in Bella Wilfer Dickens subjects Little Nell to the
test of confrontation with money and establishes through that confrontation the truth of Nell's untested intuition about the incom-

patibility of the pursuit of wealth and happiness. Where formal education, upon which the Victorian *Zeitgeist* bases itself, only fosters individual "expectation," lived education carries a conviction and an influence that is shown to be redemptive. Where Pip learns the hard way, Bella is now simply provided an example in Boffin. Dickens' art, then, seeks to arrive at those untried intuitions of the earlier fiction (with which he was then unreconciled) through lived and generative confrontations. In Bella Wilfer, then, Nell, Florence, Agnes, Esther, and Amy receive the treatment that renders them complete: the virtue that was simply posited in those women is tested in Bella through a brush with her own desiring actuality. Thus, what was essentially untried abstraction in the earlier figures is given confirmation as proven value because it emerges now from an explored descent into experience.

The experiential and aesthetic curve of Dickens' movement I have suggested is the movement from Oliver to Charley Hexam. Through the mediating figures of Nicholas, Kit Nubbles, Walter Gay, and David/Heep, Oliver is brought to full consciousness in Pip. Pip's relentless exposure to temptation and introspection yields, in turn, the rejection of Oliver in Charley Hexam. Thus, *Our Mutual Friend* may be seen as Dickens' final harvest, or the crown of his life — not as a "religious allegory" but as culminating from the enactments of all his previous work.[9] With this, however, there is a concomitant movement — the movement from Brownlow to Joe Gargery and Lizzie Hexam. Where Brownlow was an arbitrary ideal, Joe and Lizzie become the repositories of an achieved experience, figures that are not destitute (Joe has enough money to pay off £123 of Pip's debts) but that are now, somehow, seen as being socially and existentially outside the rejected bourgeois Victorian value system, outside the regulations of the "Gospel according to Podsnap." Biddy tells Pip that Joe is content to be where he is; Lizzie tells Charley that she is "very well where I am" (2.1). Yet, most curiously, it is unthinkable to Joe to stand in "Pip's way" to "honour and fortune"; and Lizzie actually pushes Charley into the Podsnap world despite Charley's fright and outrage: "You're a selfish jade . . . and you want to get rid of me." Lizzie tells her brother that by going to school and getting some "learning" he will be "much happier, and do much better"; Charley asks, "How do you know I shall?" Lizzie answers, "I don't quite know how, Charley, but I do" (1.6). Lizzie is, of course, proved quite wrong. It is a strange guilt, then (but guilt nonetheless), that attaches to Joe and Lizzie: both encourage the boys they love best (Lizzie, indeed, forces Charley) to go forth into a world that they themselves want no part of.[10]

Or is it so strange, after all? As a conclusion I suggest that the irony underlying my poser about Joe and Pip and Lizzie and Charley helps us define the limits of the dialectic in Dickens. Given the point to which Dickens arrives in *Our Mutual Friend* with respect to the Victorian bourgeoisie — the point of unequivocal rejection — Dickens has three options: (1) he can endorse the analytic assumptions of Marx and Engels, as well as the implications of those assumptions; (2) he can continue to struggle weakly and wishfully within the bourgeois Victorian *Zeitgeist*; or (3) he can take a utopian course. Clearly, Dickens does not take the first option. He does, however, will-nilly take the last two. Joe and Lizzie can think of nothing better for Pip and Charley than to hope that they might make something of the Podsnap world; Dickens, in turn, can think of nothing better than to offer Joe the utopia of the forge and Lizzie a resurrected upper-class gentleman in the pastorally utopian upper reaches of London, as though the dominating Podsnap world had simply vanished.[11] Given the parameters of Dickens' social thought and social preparedness, *Our Mutual Friend* is the farthest he can go. In a sense, then, the region of the upper Thames in his last novel defines, in its conceptual arbitrariness, a return to that region of London where Brownlow lived. In this ideological circle (as distinct from the movement of experience and art from Oliver Twist to Charley Hexam) that Dickens travels through the oeuvre, he completes the furthest possibilities of the tradition of nineteenth-century liberal-humanist thought — a tradition in which he is as inextricably bound at the end as he is at the beginning.

In his *Studies in European Liberalism* Lukács comments: "The really honest and gifted bourgeois writers who lived and wrote in the period following the great upheavals of 1848 naturally could not experience and share the development of their class with the same true devotion and intensity of feeling as their predecessors.

. . . And because in the society of their time they found nothing to support wholeheartedly . . . they remained mere spectators of the social process" (p. 141). Now Dickens wrote before as well as after 1848, and was his own predecessor. Although Lukács's encapsulated judgment has a general validity, it must be significantly amended to apply to Dickens. Before 1848 Dickens surely professes energetic sympathy with the exploited, but simultaneously, he retains, in a disabling sense, a middle-class allegiance. Of this the best evidence is his plotting. With *Dombey* — written more or less coterminously with the *Communist Manifesto* — the compromised strengths of the earlier phase find consolidation and produce a considered critique of the bourgeoisie without, as Lukács points out, yielding a socially concrete alternative. Yet, can we honestly say that after 1848 Dickens is a "mere spectator"? That characterization, in my view, is only an obvious sort of doctrinal reduction, and unresponsive, in the end, to the historical charge of Dickens' work after 1850. Marx himself attached a much finer value to the critical realism of nineteenth-century English novelists and to the subversive force of their realism:

The present splendid brotherhood of fiction writers in England, whose graphic and eloquent pages haved issued to the world more political and social truths than have been uttered by all the professional politicians, publicists and moralists put together, have described every section of the middle class from the "highly genteel" annuitant and fundholder, who looks upon all sorts of business as vulgar, to the little shopkeeper and lawyer's clerk. And how have Dickens and Thackeray, Miss Bronte and Mrs. Gaskell painted them? As full of presumption, affectation, petty tyranny and ignorance; and the civilized world have confirmed their verdict with the damning epigram that it has fixed to this class "that they are servile to those above and tyrannical to those beneath them."[12]

This contributive — that is, historically functional — critique is reflexively illuminated also in Engels' comment on Balzac:

Balzac, whom I consider a far greater master of realism than all the Zolas *passés, présents et à venir* . . . gives in a most wonderfully realistic history of French 'society', describing . . . from 1816 to 1848 the progressive inroads of the rising bourgeoisie upon the society of nobles. . . . He describes how the last remnants of this, to him, model society gradually succumbed before the intrusion of the vulgar moneyed upstart, or were corrupted by him . . . [from] this central picture . . . I have learned more than from all the professed historians, economists and statisticians of the period together.

Engels goes on to point out that although Balzac's "sympathies are all with the class doomed to extinction," his "satire is never keener, his irony never more bitter, than when he sets in motion the very men and women with whom he sympathizes most deeply.[13] Two summations may be made: (1) that, whereas Zola's naturalism is merely a mechanistic representation of reality, a historically *sterile* notation of detail, realism as in Balzac and Dickens is a historically dynamic critique, pregnant with implications for a future; and (2) that the strength of Balzac's and Dickens' critique is in perceiving the true underpinnings of the class they belong to, and in seeing the unjust and self-defeating character of its *modus operandi* — its historical *limitation*. Indeed, in this, Dickens seems totally without equivocation in *Our Mutual Friend*; Podsnappery is only to be rejected. Boffin shows that Brownlow can be threatened even by a fiction; Podsnap and Veneering complete his reality. Dickens' contribution, then, seems comparable to that of Shakespeare: Shakespeare does not endorse the new individualists, yet he is able to show us *why* a Lear, an Othello, a Timon, a Coriolanus, have had their day, *why* these figures are victims of an internal historical weakness. One would hardly think that a mean achievement.

Notes
Index

Notes

Chapter 1: Introduction

1 Wilson wrote: "We may find in Dickens' work today a complexity and a depth . . . an intellectual and artistic interest which makes Dickens loom very large in the whole perspective of the literature of the West." See Edmund Wilson, "Dickens: The Two Scrooges," in *The Wound and the Bow* (1941; rpt. New York: Oxford Univ. Press, 1954), p. 3.

2 "Mr. Dickens," James laid down, "is a great observer and a great humourist, but he is nothing of a philosopher." See Henry James, "The Limitation of Dickens," *The Nation* 1 (1865), rpt. in *The Dickens Critics*, ed. George H. Ford and Lauriat Lane, Jr. (New York: Cornell Univ. Press, 1961), p. 58.

3 The only novel where Leavis allowed Dickens' humor to be "not sentimentality" but "genius" is *Hard Times*; see F. R. Leavis, *The Great Tradition* (1948; rpt. New York: New York Univ. Press, 1967), p. 240. Leavis's retraction of his earlier estimate of Dickens dates from his essay, "*Dombey and Son*," *SR* 70 (1962): "One cannot . . . rest happily on the formula that Dickens' genius was that of a great popular entertainer: the account is not unequivocal enough" (p. 200). In 1970 Leavis could acknowledge that "Dickens was one of the greatest of

creative writers"; see F. R. Leavis and Q. D. Leavis, *Dickens the Novelist* (London: Chatto & Windus, 1960), p. ix. When I say that Leavis's selection of *Hard Times* was "understandable," I mean that as a true descendant of Matthew Arnold, Leavis's liberalism shied away from the fact of industry and tended softly, but perhaps retrogressively, towards the pastoral, "imaginative," and ultimately utopian option represented in the fluid emotion of the circus.

4 Terry Eagleton, *Criticism and Ideology* (Trowbridge and Esther: Redwood Burns, Verso ed., 1978), p. 11.

5 For example, Murray Krieger, apologist for the now old "New Criticism" and poetic "presence," shows personal hurt when he accuses Harold Bloom of having, characteristically, committed "parricide" in ganging up with the new Yale critics against the old. See Krieger, *Poetic Presence and Illusion* (Baltimore Johns Hopkins Univ. Press, 1979), pp. 113-14. Krieger's sustained defense of metaphor and the corporeality of poetic language remains, I think, valuable.

6 Stanley Fish, *Is There a Text in This Class?* (Cambridge: Harvard Univ. Press, 1980), pp. 368, 327. The anarchy implicit in Fish's position here with regard to what constitutes a "text" ought to be distinguished from a historical relativization of a "text" such as Macherey propounds: "works of art are processes . . . never produced once and for all but . . . continually susceptible to 'reproduction': in fact, they only find an identity and a content in this continual process of transformation." See P. Macherey, "Problems of Reflection," *Literature, Society, and the Sociology of Literature* (Univ. of Essex, 1977), p. 45.

Where Fish expresses a delighted subjectivity, Macherey *places* texts within larger structures of cultural endeavor. He is thus in a position to explain why authors/texts have been/are/will continue to be read differently at different historical moments and locations. Macherey's argument about "reproduction," then, releases the consensus of a wide cultural response as opposed merely to the "play" of an atomist responsibility.

7 Robert Scholes, "Who Cares about the Text?" *Novel* 17 (Winter 1984): 172-73.

8 In using here the terms *power* and *ideology* I am thinking variously of Michel Foucault and Louis Althusser. Foucault, after Nietzsche, sees all will to knowledge as will to power, accompanied by "instinct, passion, the inquisitor's devotion, cruel subtlety, and malice"; see Foucault, *Language, Counter-Memory, Practice,* trans. Donald F. Bouchard and Sherry Simon (Oxford: Blackwell, 1977), p. 162. Althusser sees ideology as the all-pervading reality at any point in history, so that "historical materialism cannot conceive that even a com-

munist society could ever do without ideology"; see Althusser, *For Marx*, trans. Ben Brewster (London: Allen Lane, Penguin Press, 1969), p. 232.

9 Ferdinand de Saussure, *Course in General Linguistics*, trans. Wade Baskin (New York: McGraw-Hill, 1959), p. 9. Emphasis added.

10 Jacques Derrida, *L'Ecriture et la différence*, quoted in Frederic Jameson, *The Prison-House of Language* (Princeton: Princeton Univ. Press, 1942), p. 186.

11 Derrida, "Structure, Sign, and Play" in *The Language of Criticism and the Sciences of Man: The Structuralist Controversy*, ed. Richard Macksey and Eugenio Donato (Baltimore: Johns Hopkins Press, 1970), pp. 250, 271–72.

12 Jameson, *Prison-House of Language*, p. 186.

13 Julia Kristeva, "D'une identité l'autre," in *Polylogue* (Paris: Seuil, 1977), p. 149; also quoted in *The Yale Critics: Deconstruction in America*, ed. Jonathan Arac et al. (Minneapolis: Univ. of Minnesota Press, 1983), p. 98.

14 Paul de Man's reading of Wordworth's "A Slumber Did My Spirit Seal" is a case in point; de Man's reading of the poem is classically New-Critical. See his "The Rhetoric of Temporality," in *Interpretation: Theory and Practice*, ed. Charles S. Singleton (Baltimore: Johns Hopkins Press, 1969), pp. 204–5. See also Murray Krieger, *Theory of Criticism* (Baltimore: Johns Hopkins Univ. Press, 1976), pp. 221–24, in which Krieger at many points successfully demonstrates that the Yale Derrideans often read literature as the New Critics did, seeing ambiguity as complexity rather than as meaninglessness.

15 Derrida, "Structure, Sign, and Play," p. 271.

16 Frederic Jameson, *The Political Unconscious* (Ithaca: Cornell Univ. Press, 1981), p. 35.

17 Frank Kermode, *The Genesis of Secrecy* (Cambridge: Harvard Univ. Press, 1979), p. 123; cf. de Man, "The Rhetoric of Temporality," where de Man reads the romantic use of symbol as ironic acknowledgment of "absence."

18 Michel Foucault, *The Archaeology of Knowledge and Discourse in Language*, trans. A. M. Sherridan Smith (New York: Harper & Row, 1976), p. 223. Foucault sees no escape from "the construction of new statements."

19 Eagleton, *Criticism and Ideology*, p. 11.

20 Jameson, *Political Unconscious*, p. 17.

21 Louis Althusser, *Lenin and Philosophy*, trans. Ben Brewster (New York: Monthly Review Press, 1971), pp. 142–86.

22 Paul de Man, "The Crisis of Contemporary Culture," *Arion* 6 (1967):

40; also in *Blindness and Insight* (New York: Oxford Univ. Press, 1971) pp. 3–19.

23 Terence Hawkes, *Structuralism and Semiotics* (Berkeley and Los Angeles: Univ. of California Press, 1977), p. 101.

24 See Edward Said, *Beginnings: Intention and Method* (New York: Basic Books, 1975; rpt. Baltimore: Johns Hopkins Univ. Press, 1978), pp. 83–84.

25 Mikhail Bakhtin, *The Dialogic Imagination*, trans. Caryl Emerson and Michael Holquist (Austin: Univ. of Texas Press, 1981), see p. 7. Bakhtin's work bids fair to revolutionize our whole view of the novel as a cultural-historical product and its intrinsically subversive tendency to devour all previous generic formations into ever new "chronotopes." A recent study that shows awareness of Bakhtin's concept of "polyphony" and Derridean "free-play" is Peter K. Garrett's *The Victorian Multiplot Novel: Studies in Dialogical Form* (New Haven: Yale Univ. Press, 1980). And yet Garrett's seems a wasted "cash-in" effort: he mentions Bakhtin cursorily, dismisses Kristeva, is unable to extricate himself from Derrida, wishes to ride over and beyond them to something new, but ends, I think, in producing only the analogical, juxtapositional defenses of multiplots that he has earlier dubbed old-fashioned and arbitrary. Example: "Oliver Twist's alternations between the worlds of Fagin and Mr. Brownlow and the Maylies disrupt linear progression and display . . . a concern with yoking contraries together, juxtaposing disparate worlds that challenge and comment on each other" (p. 25).

26 Althusser, *For Marx*, p. 62.

27 Jameson, *Political Unconscious*, p. 81.

28 Eagleton, *Criticism and Ideology*, p. 125, n. 33.

29 That Jane Austen, George Eliot, and Henry James have privileged views — always bourgeois — of these categories seems hardly in doubt. Conrad, who has always seemed an impostor in that company, is of course the most questioning and self-doubting of the so-called great-tradition novelists. The Lizzie Hexam–Eugene Wrayburn union would be unthinkable in the first three. Nor could they have given us Joe Gargery as a type of the true gentleman.

30 Günter Buck, "The Structure of Hermeneutic Experience and the Problem of Tradition," trans. Peter Heath in *New Literary History* 10 (Autumn 1978): 46.

31 See Hegel, *The Philosophy of History*, trans. J. Sibree, rev. ed. (New York: Colonial Press, 1900), p. 63. See also Ben Kimpel, *Hegel's Philosophy of History* (Boston: Student Outlines Co.), pp. 8–10, for an elucidation.

32 T. A. Jackson, *Charles Dickens: The Progress of a Radical* (New York: International Publishers, 1938), p. 11.

33 George Orwell, "Charles Dickens," in *Critical Essays* (London: Secker & Warburg, 1946), p. 7; earlier published in *Inside the Whale* (rpt. Harmondsworth: Penguin, 1969).

34 Jackson, *Dickens*, pp. 24–35. Dickens' contemporaries found this less intriguing. This is what G. M. W. Reynolds wrote in the *Weekly Newspaper* of 8 June 1851: "This wretched sycophant of Aristocracy — this vulgar flatterer of the precious hereditary peerage — is impudent enough to consider himself the people's friend! A precious friend indeed when he ridicules universal suffrage (the elementary principle of Chartism) and proclaims himself a thick and thin supporter of Lord John Russell's reform bill, even *before* he has seen it!" See N. C. Peyrouton, "Dickens and the Chartists, II," *Dkn* 60 (1964): 152–61.

35 Jackson, *Dickens*, p. 12.

36 Quoted in John Forster, *The Life of Charles Dickens*, ed. A. J. Hoppe, 2 vols. (London: J. M. Dent, 1966), 1:25. Emphasis added. Hereafter cited as Forster.

37 *The Letters of Charles Dickens*, ed. W. Dexter, 3 vols. (London: Nonesuch, 1938), 1:588.

38 Especially Raymond Williams, *Culture and Society, 1780–1850* (Harmondsworth: Penguin, 1958). The book needs to be read in its entirety for an appreciation of how "others" come to constitute the impoverished masses and "society" finds separation and elevation as "culture," presiding as a superior "court of appeal."

39 *Letters From Charles Dickens to Angela Burdett-Coutts, 1841–1865*, ed. Edgar Johnson (London: Jonathan Cape, 1963), p. 298.

40 See *Carlyle: The Nigger Question; Mill: The Negro Question* (New York: Crofts Classics, 1971), p. xxx. The Eyre controversy is a revealing case study in the context of the "two cultures" theme. All those in favor of prosecuting Eyre were scientists; those defending him were, without exception, men of letters. It is indeed a fine instance of how nineteenth-century middle-class humanism, after the 1832 Reform Bill and the consequent free-trade ethos, acquired a conservative character. Only the sociologists, biologists, geologists, and legal reformers seemed to want to carry investigations of nature and history forward. Dickens wrote to de Cerjat in 1865: "Here was a meeting of jaw bones of asses at Manchester, to censure the Jamaica Governor for his manner of putting down the insurrection. So we are badgered about New Zealanders and Hottentots, as if they were identical with men in clean shirts at Camberwell." Quoted in Michael Goldberg, *Carlyle and Dickens* (Athens: Univ. of Georgia Press, 1972), p. 147.

41 Orwell, *Critical Essays*, pp. 10, 23, 56.

42 Ibid., pp. 7, 29.

43 Williams, *Culture and Society*, p. 282.

44 See Theodor W. Adams, *Prisms*, trans. Samuel Weber and Sherry Weber (Cambridge: MIT Press, 1981), esp. pp. 17–35, an extensive discussion of the problem.

45 Althusser, *For Marx*, pp. 198–99.

46 All quotations from the autobiographical fragment are taken from Forster, 1:20–33.

47 Dickens' schoolmates seemed not to corroborate his claim of singularity. See Dr. Henry Danson's letter to Forster in the *Life*, 1: 40–41: he describes Dickens' account of Wellington Academy as "very mythical in many respects, and more especially in the compliment he pays in it to himself. I do not remember," Danson writes, "that Dickens distinguished himself in any way or carried off any prizes."

48 Althusser, *For Marx*, p. 231.

49 I use the term "differentiation" after Christopher Caudwell, *Illusion and Reality* (New York: International Publishers, 1937; rpt. 1955), pp. 36, 136, 186.

50 Sylvia Manning's contention that all Dickens' families are unhappy is, I think, misleading: see her "Families in Dickens," in *Changing Images of the Family*, ed. Virginia Tufte and Barbara Myerhoff (New Haven: Yale Univ. Press, 1979).

51 Orwell, *Critical Essays*, p. 38. Everett Knight, "The Case of Dickens," in *A Theory of the Classical Novel* (London: Routledge & Kegan Paul, 1969), pp. 106–42, echoes Orwell's static view of the self-image in Dickens within a pervasive universe of discussion which speaks of "the child" in Dickens.

52 This spatially internalized and delimited ahistorical view of Dickens and his characters was first voiced by J. Hillis Miller as a thesis: *Charles Dickens: The World of His Novels* (Bloomington: Indiana Univ. Press, 1958), at a time when Northrop Frye was the dominant critical influence on the American scene.

53 Frank Kermode, *The Classic: Literary Images of Permanence and Change* (New York: Viking, 1975), p. 140.

54 See Julia Kristeva, *Desire in Language: A Semiotic Approach to Literature and Art* (Oxford: Basil Blowell, 1980), p. 36. Kristeva's term for the interpenetration of disciplines on the literary field is "intertexuality." Whereas it may seem that "production" corresponds as a concept to the Derridean notion of "texuality," this is not really so; the idea of "production" is informed by the idea of a value-oriented

combat of counters whereas "texuality" is merely a "prison-house of language" that allows no outward referents.

55 Monroe Engel, *The Maturity of Dickens* (Cambridge: Harvard Univ. Press, 1959), p. xi. Engel offers an "investigation *first* of [Dickens'] artistic and *then* of his social beliefs" (p. xi; emphasis added), an atomistic approach that does not allow a view of the art *as* social belief. Engel's exegeses of the novels are acute and full of point. Even the converted F. R. Leavis found that the novels before *Dombey and Son* do not offer "a providently conceived whole, presenting a major theme" (Leavis and Leavis, *Dickens the Novelist*, p. xi); nevertheless, the "major theme," I wish to suggest, stretches all across Dickens.

56 Grahame Smith, *Dickens, Money, and Society* (Berkeley and Los Angeles: Univ. of California Press, 1968), p. 14.

57 John Kucich, *Excess and Restraint in the Novels of Charles Dickens* (Athens: Univ. of Georgia Press, 1981), p. 2. This echoes Monroe Engel's dichotomization of the art and social belief.

58 Eagleton, *Criticism and Ideology*, p. 129.

59 See Gabriel Pearson, "Towards a Reading of *Dombey and Son*," in *The Modern English Novel: The Reader, the Writer, and the Work*, ed. Gabriel Josipovici (New York: Barnes & Noble, 1976), p. 55. Pearson resents the whole idea of planning a novel or of pretending to move towards greater cohesion or self-knowledge.

Chapter 2: *Oliver Twist*

1 Arnold Kettle, *An Introduction to the English Novel*, 2 vols. (London: Hutchinson, 1951), 1:138, 132, 131.

2 J. Hillis Miller, *Charles Dickens: The World of His Novels* (Bloomington: Indiana Univ. Press, 1958). As a central metaphor for the novel's experience Miller isolates the "labyrinth" which "is always inward and downward . . . and never outward toward freedom" (p. 59); the freedom is ensured by the plot. Another useful reading is William T. Lankford, "The Parish Boy's Progress: The Evolving Form of *Oliver Twist*," *PMLA* 93 (1978): 20–32.

3 H. M. Daleski considers Kettle's the "best critical account of *Oliver Twist*," but also says that what happens to the poor on the street "is largely a matter of chance." He contends that Kettle blurs the "distinction between the poor and the criminal." Daleski, it seems to me, is simply not interested in the *Gestalt* within which Dickens places Oliver — the Preface — and in the end arrives only at the conviction about elect status: some poor become criminals, others do not. Daleski's attempt to depart from Kettle along these lines renders his

reading internally inconsistent; see Daleski, *Dickens and the Art of Analogy* (New York: Schocken, 1970), pp. 55, 57. Lankford, "Parish Boy's Progress," p. 32, n. 3, naively argues that Kettle "fails to distinguish plot mechanisms from the substance of the plot," and he takes seriously the "crucial struggle between Oliver's patrons and the thieves for control over the development of the boys character." Lankford, clearly, has no sense of the novel's problematic and is happy to take Dickens at his own terms in the plot.

4 John Bayley, "*Oliver Twist*: Things As They Really Are," in *Dickens and the Twentieth Century*, ed. John Gross and Gabriel Pearson (London: Routledge & Kegan Paul, 1962), pp. 49–64.

5 See Sherman Eoff, "*Oliver Twist* and the Spanish Picaresque Novel," *SP* 54 (1957): 440–47.

6 See Michael C. Kotzin, *Dickens and the Fairy Tale* (Bowling Green, Ohio: Bowling Green Univ. Popular Press, 1972), p. 50. Kathleen Tillotson writes: "Oliver was the necessary embodiment of his . . . impulse towards fairy tale and romance in his heroes and heroines"; see "*Oliver Twist*," *Essays and Studies*, n.s. 12 (1959): 92. A recent full-length study of the fairy-tale motif in Dickens is Harry Stone, *Dickens and the Invisible World: Fairy Tales, Fantasy, and Novel-Making* (Bloomington: Indiana Univ. Press, 1979); it is as well to say, though, that the book comprises many older essays.

7 See Steven Marcus, *Dickens: From Pickwick to Dombey* (New York: Basic Books, 1965), p. 80. Marcus goes on to read Oliver's passivity as a "primitive Protestant tendency" to wait for Grace: "Oliver is the *lusus naturae*, a Christian boy" (pp. 81–82). This view of Oliver is most recently echoed by Arthur Adrian, who again seems to me to put the cart before the horse: "Precisely because his goodness is innate he emerges unblemished from his rough background. His speech . . . represents that inborn goodness which can withstand the powers of darkness"; see *Dickens and the Parent-Child Relationships* (Athens, Ohio: Ohio Univ. Press, 1984), p. 79. Adrian attaches Oliver to the "pre-Adamic" tradition (p. 72). Juliet McMaster sees Fagin, Sikes, and Monks as contributing a "diabolic inversion of divine knowledge, power, and love" in a "demonic parody of the Trinity"; see "Diabolic Trinity in *Oliver Twist*," *DR* 61 (1981): 263–77. I find myself unable to rise to these readings of Oliver.

8 I find Philip Collins' view of Dickens' Christianity more acceptably in perspective than Marcus's; Collins writes: "I don't see Dickens as an agnostic, but as a rather simple Christian, much attached to what he took to be Christian ethic. . . . But I don't see . . . him, *artistically*,

as in any important way a religious writer"; see "*Dombey and Son* — Then and Now," *Dickensian* 63 (1967): 82-94. Collins' view is, I think, corroborated in Dickens' will, where he exhorts his children to follow the "New Testament in its broad spirit, and to put no faith in any man's narrow constructions of its letter here or there" (Forster, 1:283). See also Archibald C. Coolidge, "Dickens and Latitudinarian Christianity," *Dkn* 59 (1963): 57-60.

9 Forster, 1:261n.

10 Edgar Johnson has recently suggested the following view of Dickens' discipline as an artist: "I don't think that Dickens would ever have allowed anything that he wrote to get into published form unless he at least was satisfied that it was the least that he could do with it"; see "The Art of Biography: An Interview with Edgar Johnson," *DSA* 8 (1980): 1-38. He goes on to contrast Dickens in this matter with Scott, who was rather easily persuaded to make changes of one kind or another. I think Dickens, when he allowed himself to be pushed, did so only in contexts which he knew remained unaltered regardless of the compromise he was seen to make; the endings of *Great Expectations* are a case in point.

11 James R. Kincaid, "Laughter and *Oliver Twist*," *PMLA* 83 (1968): 63.

12 *Oliver Twist*, ed. Kathleen Tillotson (Oxford: Clarendon, 1966), pp. li–lxv. All citations are to this edition, indicated by chapter. Tillotson bases her text on the edition of 1846, rather than the Charles Dickens edition of 1867; see p. xl.

13 See Humphry House, *The Dickens World* (London: Oxford Univ. Press, 1941), pp. 44, 80, 216. Interestingly, Humphry House finds Dickens' description of these places as actually "less outspoken" than Kingsley's in *Alton Locke* or of Mrs. Gaskell's—a finding that supports my general argument about Dickens. In this context, Dickens' continuing refinements of language are revealing; see *Oliver Twist*, p. xxxii.

14 *Speeches of Charles Dickens*, ed. K. J. Fielding (Oxford: Clarendon, 1960), p. 129.

15 Ibid.

16 This, of course, does not either occur to or seem to bother Steven Marcus, Adrian, and others I quoted above (see n. 7). Monroe Engel's comment that "Oliver, after all, despite his misery . . . retains his innocence and . . . does no wrong" (*Maturity of Dickens*, p. 91) strikes me as uncharacteristically naive. Engel, like the others, here takes intent for achievement.

17 Marcus voices precisely this view: "Oliver's inheritance is . . . a trans-

lation of . . . spiritual and celestial reward into temporal benefits" (*Dickens: Pickwick to Dombey*, p. 84). Here Marcus is not ironic but approving.

18 *Plays by Bernard Shaw*, with a Foreword by Eric Bentley (New York: New American Library, 1960), pp. 43-45, 47-48.

19 The quoted phrase is Rosemarie Bodenheimer's; see "Dickens and the Art of Pastoral," *Centennial Review* 23 (1979): 453. Bodenheimer shows how pastoral writing "allows Dickens to evade issues of class and character" (p. 453). My only emendation would be that Oliver's language is a social "disconnection" before it is a "moral" one.

20 Forster, 1:25-26.

21 In a letter Dickens proposed to send Bentley in 1939, he writes: "The immense profits which *Oliver* has realized to its publisher, and is still realizing; the paltry, wretched, miserable sum it brought to me . . . the recollection of this, and . . . the consciousness that my books are enriching everybody connected with them but myself, and that I, with such a popularity as I have acquired, am struggling in old toils, and wasting my energies in the very height and freshness of my fame . . . to fill the pockets of others . . . all this puts me out of heart and spirits" (Forster, 1:93). At another place, while seeking Forster's approval for public readings for money, Dickens reminds Forster of that "particular relation personally affectionate and like no other man's" that he bears to his public (Forster, 2:205). This is the "fastidious class" that Dickens sets out to castigate "without reserve."

22 Forster, 1:25.

23 Graham Greene, *The Lost Childhood and Other Essays* (New York: Viking, 1951), p. 56.

24 See Philip Collins, *Dickens and Education* (1963; rpt. London: Macmillan, 1964), p. 174. Apart from Angus Wilson, Collins is the only critic who sees the importance of Dickens' treatment of child-protagonists. See particularly the chapter "Rights of Childhood." Collins is especially instructive on the children who die. Collins, however, is not engaged in tracing the dialectical structure of Dickens' art in the way that Dickens handles the self-image from novel to novel.

25 Forster, 1:25.

26 Thus the emphasis on Nancy's pursuing "eyes" as Sikes is on the run, a point made with elaboration by John Romano in *Dickens and Reality* (New York: Columbia Univ. Press, 1978), p. 133.

27 Bayley, "*Oliver Twist*," offers an illuminating discussion of the implications of Nancy's murder. The functional discrimination that he makes between crime and murder in the novel is an inspired piece of writing.

28 Steven Marcus, "Who Is Fagin?" *Commentary* 34 (1962): 48–59. Marcus here uses Dickens' formative influences with a lucid critical sensitivity which seems to get strangely warped in his discussion of the novel in *Pickwick to Dombey*. His conclusion, however, that Fagin is Oliver's father, arrived at through much convoluted reasoning, seems questionable.

29 J. Hillis Miller's argument that the underworld is threatened internally by treachery does not, in my judgment, affect the philosophical correspondence between the two "worlds." Being an extreme instance of competitive survival, treachery is likely to be only more obviously seen in the underworld, whereas in the more "legitimate" circles of officialdom, treachery is rather more effectively camouflaged. Is it not Dickens' case that the treatment given children in the workhouse — three meals of gruel a day — is treacherous to the very notion of humanness? See Miller, *Dickens*, pp. 49–50.

30 Bayley's judgment (*"Oliver Twist"*) that "the apparent contrast between Fagin's world and that of . . . Mr. Brownlow is not a real one" is bold, and I concur with reservation: only as far as Fagin as *character* represents a mythical extreme does he correspond to Brownlow, who, I argue, is an arbitrary counter to the novel's possibilities. But as a social option Brownlow remains outside of and untouched by both the Bumble and the Fagin spheres.

Chapter 3: *Nicholas Nickleby* and *The Old Curiosity Shop*

1 Mikhail Bakhtin, *Problems of Dostoevsky's Poetics*, trans. W. Rostel (Ann Arbor: Ardis, 1973), pp. 23–24.

2 Collins, *Dickens and Education*, p. 174.

3 Angus Wilson comments that "Dickens' early child heroes and heroines, being good, are . . . rewarded with slow declines into death," but that this "has no vitality in the life of the novels themselves"; see Wilson, "Dickens on Children and Childhood," in *Dickens 1970*, ed. Michael Slater (New York: Stein and Day, 1970), pp. 198, 199.

4 For a detailed account see George H. Ford, *Dickens and His Readers* (New York: Norton, 1965), pp. 55–110 and 199–227.

5 Bernard Bergonzi, in Gross and Pearson, *Dickens and the Twentieth Century*, p. 75.

6 Marcus, *Dickens: Pickwick to Dombey*, p. 125.

7 Silvère Monod, commenting on Nicholas's "Bobster! . . . That must be the servant's name" (ch. 40), suggests that "it is unthinkable that a well-born hero should fall in love with a girl whose name is at all ridiculous"; see Monod, *Dickens the Novelist* (Norman: Univ. of Oklahoma Press, 1968), p. 149.

8 Engel, *Maturity of Dickens*, p. 98.

9 Marcus notes that "their business . . . tends rapidly to be absorbed into philanthrophy" (*Dickens: Pickwick to Dombey*, p. 112). Patricia Marks good-naturedly remarks that the "Cheerybles' wealth is their good nature"; see "Time in *Nicholas Nickleby*," *VN*, no. 55 (1979): 23–26.

10 The description is Aldous Huxley's; see Ford and Lane, *The Dickens Critics*, p. 153. Ivan Melada's comment that "the benevolent eccentricity of the brothers Grant . . . equalled that of their fictional counterparts" may well be a statement of fact; it is nevertheless of no critical usefulness because it tells us nothing about the *way* Dickens employs the Cheerybles to resolve the problems of a whole culture, not to speak of his own. See Melada, *The Captain of Industry in English Fiction, 1821–1871*, (Albuquerque: Univ. of New Mexico Press, 1979), p. 108.

11 A. O. J. Cockshut, *The Imagination of Charles Dickens* (New York: New York Univ. Press, 1962), p. 88.

12 Jerome Meckier, "The Faint Image of Eden: "The Many Worlds of *Nicholas Nickleby*," *DSA* (1970): 129–46, speaks of the separate "circles" in the novel.

13 Marcus, *Dickens: Pickwick to Dombey*, p. 164.

14 Gabriel Pearson, "Quilpiad," in Gross and Pearson, *Dickens and the Twentieth Century*, p. 78.

15 See Philip Collins, "Dickens and Industrialism," *SEL 1500–1900* 20 (1980): 652. Ruskin commented in 1870: "Dickens was a pure modernist — a leader of the steam-whistle party. . . . His hero is essentially the ironmaster"; see *Dickens: The Critical Heritage*, ed. Philip Collins (London: Routledge & Kegan Paul, 1971), pp. 443–44.

16 Cockshut, *Imagination of Dickens*, p. 90.

17 Jerome Meckier comments that "Nell is destroyed by the external reality produced by the industrial revolution [meaning its harmful ecological effects], while Louisa Gradgrind will suffer because of the internal reality, the philosophical attitude behind that revolution." As I have suggested, Dickens is already aware of that philosophical attitude, although he is unable yet to render it; see Meckier's "Dickens and *King Lear*: A Myth for Victorian England," *SAQ* 71 (1972): 83.

18 A. E. Dyson, *The Inimitable Dickens: A Reading of the Novels* (London: Macmillan and St. Martin's Press, 1970), pp. 43–45.

19 Dyson's is the most spirited, even if incautiously total, modern defense of the novel: "*The Old Curiosity Shop* is the least sentimental of novels," Dyson writes. He also thinks that "it is hard to fit" the novel "into the conventional view of Dickens' development" (ibid.,

p. 23). I am not sure what is meant by "conventional view," but what I try to do is to suggest how the novel fits into the dynamics of Dickens' oeuvre.

20 Marcus, *Dickens: Pickwick to Dombey.* In Miller's view Dickens shows "that escape from the prison of the city to a divinized nature and a divinized past is identical with death" (*Dickens*, p. 95); Miller's acute observation then becomes the basis of Marcus's fine discussion. Yet, at least three recent critics have spoken positively, perhaps even glowingly, of Nell's death. John Kucich speaks of "the triumph of virtue over the grave" and, more flamboyantly, of "transcendence" embodying "the dream of an end to consciousness"; see "Death Worship among the Victorians: *The Old Curiosity Shop,*" *PMLA* 95 (1980): 58–72. Joan D. Winslow thinks Nell's death constitutes an apotheosis and an "entry into heaven"; see "*The Old Curiosity Shop*: The Meaning of Nell's Fate," *Dkn* 77 (1981): 166. Nina Auerbach believes that Nell and Agnes "exude a power beyond the human"; see *Women and the Demon: The Life of a Victorian Myth* (Cambridge: Harvard Univ. Press, 1982), p. 86.

21 Alan Douglas McKillop, *Samuel Richardson: Printer and Novelist* (Chapel Hill: Univ. of North Carolina Press, 1936), p. 169.

22 For example, in his letter to Hill (ibid., p. 131).

23 *The Correspondence of Samuel Richardson,* ed. A. L. Barbauld (London: Printed for Richard Phillips, St. Paul's Church-Yard, 1804), 4: 131. Others who shed tears were Colley Cibber and Mrs. Pilkington: see 2:128–30.

24 In a letter to Mrs. Balfour; see Austin Dobson, *Samuel Richardson* (London: Macmillan, 1902), p. 99.

25 *The Letters of Charles Dickens,* ed. Madeline House and Graham Storey, 2 (Oxford: Clarendon Press, 1969): 181–82.

26 Dyson, *Inimitable Dickens,* p. 31. Dyson is almost alone among critics of the novel to give any weight to Kit Nubbles. Although Dyson does not see how Kit functions as a surrogate to Nell, he comments that Dickens was "uneasy" about Kit and asks, "Did [Dickens] realise that though Kit is so much more valuable than Quilp, he is also much less interesting?" (p. 34).

27 Julian Moynahan, "The Hero's Guilt: The Case of *Great Expectations,*" *Essays in Criticism* 10 (1960): 60–79. Moynahan's is a brilliant demonstration, but my interest in deflected images is to entirely different purposes.

28 *Letters,* ed. House and Storey, 2:160.

29 Warrington Winters notes that only ten men are present at Nell's funeral—Mrs. Garland has arrived earlier but is not present—and asks "Shall we say that Dickens here excluded his mother from his

own funeral?" See "A Consummation Devoutly to be Wished," *Dkn* 63 (1967): 176–78.

30 Ross H. Dabney, *Love and Property in the Novels of Dickens* (Berkeey and Los Angeles: Univ. of California Press, 1967), p. 21.

31 Mark Spilka suggests a psychoanalytic interpretation of this exhaustion: "The lavish flow of tears over Nell and her counterparts, was a form of cultural neurosis in the audience, a kind of mass indulgence in erotic feeling, in the name of perfect goodness"; see Spilka, "Little Nell Revisited," *Papers of the Michigan Academy of Science, Arts, and Letters* 45 (1960): 427–37.

Chapter 4: *Martin Chuzzlewit*

1 Daleski, *Dickens and the Art of Analogy*, p. 83.

2 Ibid., pp. 89–90.

3 Some critics of Dickens feel quite happy at once with the "Dickens [who] slowly unfolds causality" and gives us, simultaneously, "saintlike and intact idea[s] that resisted any idea of environmental pressure"; see Barbara Hardy, "The Complexity of Dickens," in Slater, *Dickens 1970*, pp. 40, 42.

4 Daleski, *Dickens and the Art of Analogy*, p. 110.

Chapter 5: *Dombey and Son*

1 Kathleen Tillotson, *Novels of the Eighteen-Forties* (1954; rpt. Oxford: Clarendon, 1971).

2 Forster, 2:20.

3 Philip Collins, "*Dombey and Son* — Then and Now," *Dkn* 63 (1967): 82–94.

4 Henri Talon, "*Dombey and Son*: A Closer Look at the Text," *DSA* 1 (1970): 157. The apotheosis of this view of *Dombey and Son* is Harry Stone's more recent view: "With *Dombey*, for the first time in a Dickens novel, the fairy tale has become a consistent and pervasive force"; see Stone, *Dickens and the Invisible World*, p. 146. My own view is, of course, the opposite — that with *Dombey* the fairy tale in Dickens begins to be, not "pervasive," but residual.

5 Johnson, *Dickens to Burdett-Coutts*, p. 299.

6 *Letters*, ed. Dexter, 2:695, to MacCready.

7 *Household Words*, vol. 11 (3 Feb. 1855), and vol. 12 (4 Aug. 1855). See also "Our Commission," *Household Words*, vol. 12 (11 Aug. 1855).

8 See, in *Household Words*, "Twenty Shillings in the Pound," vol. 16 (7 Nov. 1857); "Bankruptcy in Six Easy Lessons," vol. 17 (13 Feb. 1958); and "My Model Director," vol. 19 (26 Feb. 1859). In *All the Year Round*, "Pay for Your Places," vol. 4 (27 Oct. 1860); and "Money

or Merit?" vol. 3 (21 April, 1860). I am indebted to Monroe Engel for pointing me to this material.

9 *Speeches,* ed. Fielding, p. 106.

10 Tillotson, *Novels of the Eighteen-Forties,* p. 177. The phrases are quotations which the writer says she has been unable to trace.

11 See Raymond Williams, "Dickens and Social Ideas," in Slater, *Dickens 1970,* pp. 77–98. John Romano's comment, "We have in Dombey an individual who represents within himself his society's own concatenation of ills, private and public," seems to me apt. See Romano, *Dickens and Reality,* p. 143.

12 Discussions of the Railroad in *Dombey and Son* have, on the whole, tended to be confused and confusing, either because they are one-sided or, more importantly, because they fail to connect Dickens' perception of the Railroad with his perception of Dombeyism. Thus, for Steven Marcus there is no "ambiguity" about Dickens being totally in favor of change, so that the Railroads are a necessary and beneficial "cataclysm of nature"; see Marcus, "The English Dickens and *Dombey and Son,*" in *Dickens Centennial Essays,* ed. Ada Nisbet and Blake Nevius (Berkeley and Los Angeles: Univ. of California Press, 1971), pp. 1–21. The best discussion I know of is Harland S. Nelson's "Staggs' Gardens: The Railway through Dickens' World," *DSA* 3 (1974): 41–53. Nelson concludes that Dickens "was recording what he saw . . . which was a disquiet that he could not put a name to." My argument is that Dickens' "disquiet" is not caused by the Railway *per se,* but by the quality of the human impetus which he perceives to be informing it. I think Terry Eagleton is facile in his observation that "the famous railways scene exhilaratedly affirms bourgeois industrial progress at the same time that it protests . . . against it on behalf of the petty-bourgeoisie whom it dooms to obsolescence"; see Eagleton, "Ideology and Literary Form," *NLR* 90 (1975): 90. As I argue, Dickens' logic here is an emotional logic and does not follow class lines.

13 Marcus remarks perceptively on tone and language in the novel; see *Dickens: Pickwick to Dombey,* pp. 292–96. The most thorough examination of the workings of the novel's allusions, recurring motifs, and especially its symbolism of the sea is to be found in William Axton, "Tonal Unity in *Dombey and Son,*" *PMLA* 78 (1964): 341–48.

14 Forster, 2:20, 23.

15 Spilka argues that the relationship between Florence and Paul, "grounded in the affection Dickens felt for his sister Fanny, and for . . . Mary Hogarth," suggests "unwitting incest"; see *Dickens and Kafka* (Bloomington: Indiana Univ. Press, 1963), p. 51.

16 Forster, 2: 36.

17 F. R. Leavis comments: "That Dickens changed his mind about Walter Gay and, instead of letting him go to the bad, brought him back to marry Florence, also made no difference that mattered"; see "Dombey and Son," SR 70 (1962): 177-201.

Chapter 6: David Copperfield

1 Miller, Charles Dickens, p. 151. See also Ruth Ashby, "David Copperfield's Story-Telling in the Dark," DSN 9 (1978): 81.

2 This forgiving phraseology is from Gwendolyn Needham, "The Undisciplined Heart of David Copperfield," NCF 9 (1954): 81-107. Since I quote extensively from Needham, I do not footnote further references as I proceed. Her article may be read in its entirety to assess the justice or otherwise of what I say.

3 Joseph Gold, Charles Dickens: Radical Moralist (Minneapolis: Univ. of Minnesota Press, 1972), p. 178.

4 In a rather peculiarly structured book which gives 85 pages to David Copperfield, 40 pages to Edwin David, and 25 pages to the rest of Dickens, Bert G. Hornback waxes lyrical over the management of "cadence" in David's poser as to whether he is or is not the "hero of my life"; see "The Hero of My Life" (Athens: Ohio Univ. Press, 1981), pp. 14-15. He sees David as not only superior in imagination and comprehension to Raskolnikov but also thinks of "David's heroism" as "more important than that of Oedipus, or Lear or Faust" (p. 56). Hornback's is clearly a case of devotion. Indeed, the only parallel he can find in "our culture's history" is Dante (p. 64, n. 6). I have no idea what Hornback means.

5 The Haunted Man also falls within this period, and the figure of Redlaw projects closely Dickens' retrospectives of this time. See Edgar Johnson, Charles Dickens: His Tragedy and Triumph, 2 vols. (New York: Simon and Schuster, 1952), 2:656-60.

6 Forster, 1:32.

7 Johnson, Dickens to Burdett-Coutts, p. 135.

8 Cockshut, Imagination of Dickens, p. 115; see also Arnold Kettle, "Thoughts on David Copperfield," REL 2 (1961): 65-74.

9 Forster, 2:76; Forster also wrote that "it would be the greatest mistake to imagine . . . the identity of the fictitious novelist with the real one" and that David ought to be studied more in his "unlikeness" than "likeness to Dickens" (2:105). My argument is that the likeness and the unlikeness ought to be viewed dialectically.

10 John Lucas, The Melancholy Man (London: Methuen, 1970), p. 168.

11 Janet H. Brown, "The Narrator's Role in David Copperfield," DSA

2 (1972): 197–207, does well to isolate the self-absorbed character of David's narrative voice. I differ with her in two respects: (1) I do not think Dickens is in this novel as much in control of our responses as Ms. Brown supposes, and (2) when Ms. Brown says that "we are required in this novel to recognize . . . willingly" David's view of things or else "to put the book down" she asks us, in effect, to acquiesce in the "severely limited" narrative intelligence (p. 203). I think it is useless to pretend that the reader has only as much freedom as David will grant him. Felicity Hughes, in speaking of the problem of spaced awarenesses in the novel, finds Dickens' comment on David "disquieting"; see "Narrative Complexity in *David Copperfield*," *ELH* 41 (1974): 89–105. I often find the *absence* of such comment "disquieting."

12 Edmund Wilson thought David Copperfield a "holiday"; see "Dickens: The Two Scrooges," in *The Wound and the Bow*, p. 43. I am encouraged that Geoffrey Thurley makes much the same point; see *The Dickens Myth: Its Genesis and Structure* (Routledge and Kegan Paul: London, 1976), p. 133. Leonard F. Manheim comments: "David Copperfield is Dickens' greatest *Bildungsroman* . . . balked and frustrated at every turn"; see "The Personal History of David Copperfield," *AI* 9 (1952): 41. See also his "The Dickens Hero as Child," *SNNTS* 1 (1969): 189–95.

13 Mark Spilka, *Dickens and Kafka: A Mutual Interpretation* (Bloomington: Indiana Univ. Press, 1963), pp. 138–49.

14 Carl Baudelin, "David Copperfield: A Third Interesting Penitent," *SEL 1500–1900* 16 (1978): 606. Baudelin demonstrates perceptively that at several points in the action of the novel David wills events subliminally and is shocked by their actual realization.

15 Lucas, *Melancholy Man*, p. 197.

16 Raymond Williams shows how the "ladder" becomes a perfect symbol for bourgeois definitions of progress: only one can go up at a time, leaving the group behind; see *Culture and Society*, p. 317.

17 J. R. Kincaid, "The Darkness of *David Copperfield*," *Di S* 1 (1965): 65–75. See also his "Symbol and Subversion in *David Copperfield*," *SNNTS* 1 (1969): 196–206.

18 Angus Wilson — who has, in my view, the finest perception of the play of Dickens' self-images — also tends to see David within a structure of extenuation when he comments that "David is the culmination . . . of these purely genteel heroes"; see his "Heroes and Heroines of Dickens," *REL* 2 (1961): 9–18. Ruth Ashby, "David Copperfield's Story-Telling," p. 81, echoes Kincaid in her comment that David often retreats behind a fictive persona. More especially, John P. McGowan argues that since memory is only another form of realism, in that it

seeks to recall the object *as it was*, David moves from memory to "fancy" in order to substitute fictive ideals; see *"David Copperfield*: The Trial of Realism," *NCF* 34 (1979): 1–19.

19 This view of David's *arrival*, of the meaning of the whole narrative, has, as I said earlier, been pervasive after Needham. Thus, Albert A. Dunn writes: "David must recognize his past errors and delusions" before he is "joined with Agnes"; see "Time and Design in *David Copperfield*," *E & S* 59 (1978): 227. J. M. Reibetanz similarly concludes that David achieves heroism at last when he makes his statement to Agnes — freeing her from obligation — without any "alloy of self," and finds reward in union with her; see "Villain, Victim, and Hero: Structure and Theme in *David Copperfield*," *DR* 59 (1979): 321–27. In my view, Reibetanz's conclusion disables an otherwise acute analysis of the real heroes in the novel in various crisis contexts, none of which reflect flatteringly on David.

20 Reibetanz, "Villain, Victim, and Hero," p. 325.

21 Cockshut, *Imagination of Dickens*, p. 119.

22 Felicity Hughes, "Narrative Complexity in *David Copperfield*," p. 103, believes Steerforth's ascendance over David a case of "hypnotism" or "magnetism" — another instance of how often the Dickens critic opts for the fairy tale in preference to the obvious.

23 In contrast David notices later on that the street where Traddles lived with the Micawbers "was not as desirable a one as I could have wished it to be" (ch. 27).

24 Manheim asks: "Can it . . . be that there is something fascinating about Steerforth's failure to apotheosize the glories of virginity, something that David-Dickens longs for, but can never hope to attain? Or is it conceivable that David sees in Steerforth a means of satisfying the cravings of Eros without the necessity of soiling any virgins?" ("Personal History of David Copperfield," p. 33). Baudelin sees Steerforth straightforwardly as David's surrogate in the business of ravishing Emily ("David Copperfield," p. 606).

25 See Martin C. Battestin, *The Moral Basis of Fielding's Art: A Study of Joseph Andrews* (1959; rpt. Middletown Conn.: Wesleyan Univ. Press, 1964), for a full account of the Latitudinarian position as represented by preachers like Tillottson and Clark.

26 Chapter 50 contains perhaps the most heartless instance of David's callousness; David conceals himself while Rosa Dartle lashes out at his returned childhood sweetheart, Emily, with merciless cruelty. See Dyson, *Inimitable Dickens*, pp. 139–49, for a full treatment of the David-Emily context.

27 Ibid., p. 148; Johnson, *Dickens: Tragedy and Triumph*, 2:699.

28 Lucas, *Melancholy Man*, p. 170.

29 Cockshut, *Imagination of Dickens*, p. 119.

30 Barbara Hardy, *The Moral Art of Dickens* (London: Athlone, 1970), p. 135.

31 Manheim, "Personal History of David Copperfield," p. 32. Keith Carabine makes a fairly direct statement of surrogacy: "Heep embodies and deflects those elements of David which the new perspective demands he deny—namely his ambition and sexuality." Yet he makes scant use of that perception in reading the novel. See Carabine, "Reading in *David Copperfield*," in *Reading the Victorian Novel*, ed. Ian Gregor (New York: Barnes and Noble, 1980), p. 161. Loralee Mac-Pike sees David's growth as contingent upon his adjustment with his "three contemporaries," Steerforth, Traddles, and Heep; see *Dostoevsky's Dickens: A Study of Literary Influence* (London: Gregor Prior, 1981), p. 123. In a sense, the most extended comment on Heep is in Harry Stone, "Dickens and Fantasy: The Case of Uriah Heep," *Dkn* 75 (1979): 95–103, in which Stone provides exhaustive commentary on Heep's fairy-tale attributes, David's fantasies about him, Dickens' use of grotesque and biblical imagery in presenting him, and so forth. While Stone is so enraptured by these aspects of Heep that much of the more directly social comment he offers seems lost in a gothic blaze, his account nonetheless supersedes everything else I know. The article is incorporated in his *Dickens and the Invisible World*.

32 Heep is therefore not simply "a clear-cut reversion to an earlier melodramatic theme," as Ross H. Dabney comments in *Love and Property in the Novels of Dickens*, p. 69. Elsewhere (p. 76) Dabney comments more perceptively that "David is a new kind of Dickens hero, one who developed some of the grim confidence, method and will hitherto reserved to Dickens' villains." For a contrast, J. Hillis Miller writes of David's success—and of the fates of the other characters—that "his destiny and identity and those of other people have been made by a metaphysical power, the power of divine Providence" (*Charles Dickens*, p. 156). Providence shapes not just life and art but literary criticism as well.

Chapter 7: The Novels of the Fifties

1 There are many excellent discussions of *Bleak House* and *Little Dorrit*. I have benefitted particularly from my reading of James R. Brown, *Dickens: Novelist in the Market Place* (London: Macmillan, 1982).

2 See Barbara Lecker, "The Split Character of Charles Dickens," *E & S* 62, no. 5 (1981): 429–41, for a fuller account of this pattern.

3 Joseph A. Kestner writes: "Both conclusions intend a physical part-

ing, but with a spiritual unity, between Pip and Estella" on the basis that "in the revised conclusion . . . the final phrase is 'friends apart'"; see *The Spatiality of the Novel* (Detroit: Wayne State Univ. Press, 1978), p. 186, n. 66. I offer more elaborate comment on the ending of *Great Expectations* in my next chapter.

Chapter 8: *Great Expectations*

1 Forster, 2:285.

2 Christopher Ricks, "*Great Expectations*," in Gross and Pearson, *Dickens and the Twentieth Century*, pp. 199–211.

3 I cannot say if this is what Barry Westburg also means to suggest when he says that "*Great Expectations* confesses itself as a fiction about fiction-making, and in this sense it is self-critical"; see *The Confessional Fictions of Charles Dickens* (DeKalb: Northern Illinois Univ. Press, 1977), p. xvii, Westburg's rather too self-consciously and heavily laden use of the New Critical idiom does not always help. It is not clear from his account why *Great Expectations* is a "fiction about fiction-making."

4 I enjoyed very much the rather unfairly neglected article by Mordecai Marcus and feel him kindred in the quality of attention I propose to give the novel; see his "Pattern of Self-Alienation in *Great Expectations*," *VN* 26 (1964): 9–12.

5 Dorothy VanGhent comments that "there is, perhaps, no purer expression of solipsism in literature"; see *The English Novel: Form and Function* (New York: Rinehart, 1953), p. 126. My argument is that it is the sureness of Joe's self-knowledge which at once makes him the most empathic character in the novel.

6 Max Byrd makes a similar point, although he is not concerned with the existential significance of Joe's reading of himself; see "Reading in *Great Expectations*," *PMLA* 91 (1976): 259–65.

7 *Wuthering Heights* (New York: Random House, 1960); cited in my text as *WH* with page number.

8 Kettle, *An Introduction to the English Novel*, 1:139–55.

9 In a general argument about the "beleaguered self" in Dickens' novels, Richard Barickman comments that Joe turns "conversational occasions into self-aggrandizing or self-protective monologues"; see "The Comedy of Survival in Dickens' Novels," *Novel* 11 (1978): 129. I cannot imagine a less sensitive response to Dickens' whole purpose — dramatized purpose — in the uniquely eloquent linguistic disability he gives to Joe. In my view, Dickens' art here attempts to produce a transparent sincerity, a total lack of subterfuge and glibness, which makes Joe the sort of hero that Carlyle thinks Cromwell to have been. I may

add that the whole point of the Satis House meeting is to communicate Joe's hurt that Pip should stand there and think either that Havisham's questions need to be asked or that Joe can have more than one answer. In that sense, it is only right that Joe should be talking to Pip rather than to Havisham.

10 Ursula LeGuin offers a comprehensive contemporary statement of the problematic: "If you deny any affinity with another person . . . if you declare it to be wholly different from yourself . . . as men have done to women, and class has done to class, and nation has done to nation — you may hate it or deify it; but in either case you have denied its . . . equality, and its human reality. You have made it into a thing, to which the only possible relationship is a power relationship. And you have fatally impoverished your own reality. You have, in fact, alienated yourself." See LeGuin, "American Science Fiction and the Other," *Science Fiction Studies* 2 (1975): 209.

11 Christopher Ricks, "*Great Expectations*," in Gross and Pearson, *Dickens and the Twentieth Century*, p. 203.

12 Miller, *Charles Dickens*, p. 66.

13 Geoffrey Thurley focuses sharply on the social achievement of the novel when he comments that in embracing Magwitch, Pip finally embraces his own proletarian past; see *The Dickens Myth*, p. 303. Thurley's, in my view, is the best single account of the novel, in spite of his eccentric view that the novel has nothing to do with snobbishness.

14 Martin Meisel, "The Ending of *Great Expectations*," *Essays in Criticism* 15 (1965): 326–31.

15 Milton Milhauser, "*Great Expectations*: The Three Endings," *DSA* 2 (1972): 267–77. A. L. French provides a painstakingly ingenious computation of dates and of Pip's age at various stages of the narrative and concludes that since Pip is fifty-four when he comes back from the East, the only right ending for the novel is the "parting"; see "Old Pip: The Ending of *Great Expectations*," *Essays in Criticism* 29 (1979): 257–60. Edgar Rosenberg provides a comprehensive history of the endings debate in "Last Word on *Great Expectations*: A Textual Brief on the Six Endings," *DSA* 9 (1981): 87–115.

16 In an eloquent phrase, Jack Lindsay calls Pip "the emblem of the age"; see *Charles Dickens* (New York: Philosophical Library, 1950), p. 371. Daleski, on the contrary, asserts that "there is nothing in the text, not a word, or a phrase, or an image, which indicates that Pip has the sort of representative significance suggested" (*Dickens and the Art of Analogy*, p. 238. It is instructive that a critic as alert as Daleski can here have so badly missed the mark. Westburg's emphasis, determin-

edly, is on the fictive and the aesthetic. He finds the novel "ethically neutral, messageless about life, and yet still significant as an aesthetic confession, a confession about, and by means of art" (*Confessional Fictions of Dickens*, p. 180). Whereas this is certainly wrong about *Great Expectations*, it is demonstrably right about some evaluations of it.

Chapter 9: *Our Mutual Friend*

1 References are to book and chapter of *Our Mutual Friend*.

2 Jackson writes: "Class-contrast and class-antagonism, class-hatred and class-contempt, are woven into the innermost texture of *Our Mutual Friend*" (*Charles Dickens*, p. 204). Kettle endorses this judgment; see his *"Our Mutual Friend,"* in Gross and Pearson, *Dickens and the Twentieth Century*, p. 214.

3 Kettle again delimits and demarcates the social situation here acutely; the question, he argues, is "not of money as such but of values." Kettle, *"Our Mutual Friend,"* p. 216.

4 P. J. M. Scott likes to believe that in Bradley Headstone "the issue has gone far beyond . . . all questions of social criticism," whatever that means; see *Reality and Comic Confidence in Charles Dickens* (London: Macmillan, 1979), pp. 45–46. It has generally, of course, been the critical emphasis to see Headstone as an entirely strange creation whose interest must be seen to be purely — and mysteriously — psychological and criminological. We are to understand this purity as being unrelated to society, social reality, social criticism, and so forth.

5 Robert S. Baker provides a full reading of the theme of education in the novel; see "Imagination and Literacy in Dickens' *Our Mutual Friend*," *Criticism* 18 (1976): 57–72.

6 Rosemary Mundhenk makes the point that one of Dickens' very effective dramatic strategies is to limit the reader's awareness about Boffin to that of Bella Wilfer; in this way, the reader is educated coterminously with her. See "The Education of the Reader in *Our Mutual Friend*," *NCF* 34 (1979): 41–58.

7 Of Bella's situation Kettle writes that her "mercinariness" is "unlike the mercinariness of Podsnappery . . . hers is a working-class mercinariness, not much different in essence from that of Richardson's Pamela, based simply on the bitter experience of what not having money involves" (*"Our Mutual Friend,"* p. 215).

8 Jack Lindsay comments that "the picture of the perversion through wealth has been too true, too effectively done. In point of fact we feel two Boffins." See *Charles Dickens*, p. 382.

9 Thurley writes that *Our Mutual Friend* "has a quality which can hardly

be compared with any earlier Dickens novel." The phrase "religious allegory" is his (*The Dickens Myth*, p. 305).

10 Kettle's argument that "these people despite their poverty, decline to 'rise' by grasping 'opportunities' that will undermine their humanity" (*"Our Mutual Friend*," p. 218), if anything, points only to the irony of the problematic here; the fact is that they are unable to conceive of an alternative to "rising" where it concerns Pip and Charley Hexam.

11 See Annabel M. Patterson's *"Our Mutual Friend*: Dickens as the Compleat Angler," *DSA* 1 (1970): 252-64, for an excellent discussion of the two-part structure of the novel, defined by the upper and lower Thames. Patterson sees the upper region as "pastoral."

12 *Marx and Engels on Literature and Art*, ed. Lee Baxandall and Stefan Morawski (St. Louis and Milwaukee: Telos, 1973), p. 105.

13 See *Marxists on Literature: An Anthology*, ed. David Craig (Harmondsworth: Penguin, 1975), pp. 270-71.

Index

Adrian, Arthur, 148n7, 149n16
Agamemnon, 103
Alice (*Dombey and Son*), 69, 74
All the Year Round, 25, 64–65
Althusser, Louis, 13, 142n8
Arnold, Matthew, 12, 142n3
Austen, Jane, 89, 144n29

Bagstock, Joe (*Dombey and Son*), 65–66
Bakhtin, Mikhail, 8, 36, 144n25
Balzac, Honoré de, 133, 137–38
Barickman, Richard, 160n9
Barkis (*David Copperfield*), 101
Barnaby Rudge, 11
Barthes, Roland, 4
Bates, Charley (*Oliver Twist*), 34–35
Baudelin, Carl, 81
Bayley, John, 22, 26, 151n30
Bedwin, Mrs. (*Oliver Twist*), 37, 43
Beggar's Opera, 24
Bergonzi, Bernard, 40, 44
Biddy (*Great Expectations*), 108, 113, 117–18, 127–28, 135
Blacking-factory and Dickens' boyhood, 13–16, 95, 121, 129
Bleak House, 16, 26, 101–6, 110
Bloom, Harold, 142n5
Boffin, Nicodemus (*Our Mutual Friend*), 130–31, 135, 138
Bradshaigh, Lady, 53
Brass, Sally (*The Old Curiosity Shop*), 46, 55–56, 63
Brass, Sampson (*The Old Curiosity Shop*), 46, 55–56, 63

Bray, Madeline (*Nicholas Nickleby*), 42, 45
Brontë, Emily, 114
Brown, Mrs. (*Dombey and Son*), 74, 103
Brownlow (*Oliver Twist*), 21, 27, 29–30, 33–35, 37, 52, 56, 59, 63, 66, 76, 79, 91, 122
Buck, Günter, 9, 144n30
Bucket, Inspector (*Bleak House*), 104
Bulwer-Lytton, E. G. E. L., 105
Bumble (*Oliver Twist*), 33–35, 55, 110
Burdett-Coutts, Angela, 64

Capitalism: and class distinction, contrast and antagonism of, 67, 130–38; in *David Copperfield*, 81–82, 92–101; in *Great Expectations*, 108–29; and industrial revolution, 46–57; and marriage and Victorian values, 103, 105–6; practices of, in *Dombey and Son*, 62–76; and social reforms, 11–13
Carker, James (*Dombey and Son*), 66, 69–70, 102
Carlyle, Thomas, 11–12, 53, 77, 145n40
Carstone, Richard (*Bleak House*), 45, 103
Carton, Sydney (*A Tale of Two Cities*), 105
Chartists, 11
Cheeryble, Charles (*Nicholas Nickleby*), 42, 44–46, 56, 60, 91

Cheeryble, Frank (*Nicholas Nickleby*), 45

Cheeryble, Ned (*Nicholas Nickleby*), 42, 44–46

Childhood, growth from, 77–101

Children: as autobiographical characters, 108–29; death of, 36–39, 41, 46–57; exploitation of, 21–39, 41, 46–57, 62–76

Christian ethics, 21–35

A Christmas Carol, 15

Chuzzlewit, Anthony, 58–59

Chuzzlewit, Martin (elder), 30, 58–62

Chuzzlewit, Martin (younger), 16, 39, 59–61, 63

Clarissa, 53

Class distinctions, 67, 130–38; in *David Copperfield*, 81–82, 92–101; in *Dombey and Son*, 64, 66; in *Our Mutual Friend*, 130–38; and social reform, 11–13

Clennam, Arthur (*Little Dorrit*), 16, 103, 106–7

Cockshut, A. O. J., 85, 97

Collins, Philip, 37–38, 64, 68, 148*n8*, 150*n24*

Combination Acts in 1825, 11

Communism, 130–38

Communist Manifesto, 137

Compeyson (*Great Expectations*), 110, 124–25

Conrad, Joseph, 144*n29*

Conscious intentions and unconscious forces, 24–25, 27

Contradictions in Dickens, 22–23, 27, 36–57, 62–76

Copperfield, David, 13–14, 16, 32, 76, 102, 106–9, 117, 122, 128–29; and price of success, 77–101

Copperfield, Dora (Spenlow), 77, 80–83, 93, 98–101

Cordelia (*King Lear*), 52, 70

Corruption in big business and government, 64–66

Cratchit family (*A Christmas Carol*), 15

Creakle, Mr. (*Nicholas Nickleby*), 84, 86–88

Creakle, Miss (*Nicholas Nickleby*), 84

Crewler, Sophy (*David Copperfield*), 82

Criminality, 24–25, 30, 33–35

Crummles, Mrs. Vincent (*Nicholas Nickleby*), 41

Crummles, Vincent (*Nicholas Nickleby*), 41

Cuttle (*Dombey and Son*), 63, 73, 76

Daleski, H. M., 58–60, 147*n3*

Danson, Henry, 146*n47*

Dartle, Rosa (*David Copperfield*), 88–89, 91

David Copperfield, 10, 32, 120; capitalism and class distinction in, 81–82, 92–101; impact of death in, 80–81, 87, 90, 101; economics and price of success in, 77–101; educational values in, 80, 84, 86–89, 91–92; first person narrative in, 14; growth of character in, 77–101; mother image in, 78–79, 87–88, 92–95, 98, 100; romantic associations in, 77, 80–83, 87–88, 90–91, 93, 98–101; surrogate relations in, 81–91, 96–97, 99–101; women influencing character in, 77–83, 87–88, 90, 92, 98–101

Death: of child characters, 36–39, 41, 46–57; impact of, 80–81, 87, 90, 101

De Man, Paul, 7, 143*nn14, 17, 22*

Derrida, Jacques, 5–7, 143*nn10–11, 15*

De Saussure, Ferdinand, 5, 143*n9*

Dick (*Oliver Twist*), 16, 30, 32, 36, 50, 52–53, 56–57, 75, 79, 100

Dickens, Charles:
in blacking-factory and boyhood, 13–16, 95, 121, 129
on value of breeding, 77–101
capitalism, class distinction and social reform in works of, 11–

13, 46–57, 62–76, 77–101, 108–29, 130–38
character similarities in works of, 10, 52, 108, 135–36
and Christian ethics, 21–35
and class distinctions, 11–13, 62–76, 81–82, 92–101, 130–38
conscious intentions and unconscious forces in, 24–25, 27
contradictions in works of, 22–23, 27, 36–57, 62–76
and corruption in big business, 64–66
and depiction of criminality, 24–25, 30, 33–35
economics in works of, 46–57, 62–76, 77–101, 108–29
educational values of, 25–26, 80, 84, 86–89, 91–92, 112–13, 115–16, 120, 133, 135
father image in works of, 50–52, 55, 57, 63, 70, 119–29
and first person narrative, 14
and government in Victorian England, 62–76
and greed, 58–76
finds human value in human relatedness, 108–29
ideology of, 4–10, 12, 17, 24–25, 28–29, 62–101
marriage and Victorian values in works of, 64, 65, 68, 103, 105–6
martyrdom in, 36–57, 62, 71, 75
and military-industrial complexes, 65–66
moral allegories of, and moral survival, 62–101
mother image of, 78–79, 87–88, 92–95, 98, 101
Parliament, distrust of, 64–65
and plot and pattern in *Oliver Twist*, 21–27, 30–32
and railroads and business practices, 65, 69–70, 75
and religion, 23, 25–26, 33, 49, 53

and romantic associations, 49–51, 77, 80–83, 87–88, 90–91, 93, 98–101
self-awareness and image in works of, 9, 16–17, 34–57, 62–101, 108–38
and slum clearance, 21–35
social being and adjustment, 22–23, 26–27, 29, 31, 33, 35
as social critic, 10
and social mores, 46–57
social perceptions of, 62–76
and social reality in human relatedness, 127
and social reform, 11–13
surrogate relations in works of, 39–47, 50–52, 57, 62–63, 81–91, 96–97, 99–101
unconscious forces and conscious intentions of, 24–25, 27
Victorian society and values in works of, 46–57, 62–76, 103–106
Dickens, Elizabeth, 95
Dickens, Fanny, 15–16
Dickens, John, 95
Dodger, The Artful (*Oliver Twist*), 16, 25, 28, 31, 34
Dombey, Florence, 16, 39, 69–71, 73, 75–76, 105, 135
Dombey, Mr., 59, 103, 131
Dombey, Paul, 16, 31, 38, 39, 52, 66–76, 79, 100, 102
Dombey and Son, 15–16, 27, 30, 37–39, 49–51, 58, 78–79, 102, 104, 137; capitalism in, 67, class distinctions in, 64, 66; corruption and big business in, 64–66; distrust of Parliament in, 64–65; father-son relations in, 62–76; fortune hunters in, 63–76; marriage in, 66; martyrdom in, 62, 75; moral allegories of, 64, 68; self-image in, 62–63; social perceptions of, 62–64; surrogate relations in, 63; Victorian values in, 63, 65–66, 68
Dombeyism, 62–76, 102

Dorrit, Amy, 16, 52, 76, 105-7, 135
Dostoevsky, Fyodor, 8-9, 36
Dotheboys Hall, 40, 42
Drummle, Bentley (*Great Expectations*), 108
Dyson, E. A., 51, 152*nn18-19*, 153*n26*

Eagleton, Terry, 3, 8, 19, 22, 142*n4*, 155*n12*
Earnshaw, Cathy (*Wuthering Heights*), 113-14
Economic influences and system, 62-76; in *Great Expectations*, 108-29; in *The Old Curiosity Shop*, 46-57; and price of success, 77-101
Edith (*Dombey and Son*), 66, 69, 74, 103
Educational values, 25-26, 80, 84, 86-89, 91-92, 112-13, 115-16, 120, 133, 135; Victorian view of, 104
Eliot, George, 12, 144*n29*
Eliot, T. S., 47, 104
Engel, Monroe, 19, 147*n55*, 149*n16*
Engels, Friedrich, 67, 130, 136-38
Estella (*Great Expectations*), 105, 111, 113-15, 117-18, 121-23, 127
Eyre controversy, 12, 145*n40*

Fagin, Bob (*Oliver Twist*), 14-16, 25, 33-35, 38, 55, 119, 125-26
Father image, 50-52, 55, 57, 63, 70, 119-29
Father-son relations, 62-76
Fielding, Henry, 94
Fish, Stanley, 4, 142*n6*
Flaubert, Gustave, 134
Forster, John, 11-13, 23, 30, 54, 56, 62, 76, 78-79, 108
Fortune hunters, 58-60, 62-76
Foucault, Michel, 142*n8*, 143*n18*

Gambling, 51, 55
Gamfield (*Oliver Twist*), 32, 34

Gargery, Joe (*Great Expectations*), 63, 106, 108-9, 113, 116-17, 132-33, 135-36; as father image, 119, 122, 124
Gargery, Mrs. Joe (*Great Expectations*), 111-12
Gay, John, 24
Gay, Walter (*Dombey and Son*), 16, 39, 73, 76, 100, 102, 105, 135
Gills, Sol (*Dombey and Son*), 73, 76
Gradgrind, Louisa (*Hard Times*), 76
Gradgrind, Thomas (*Hard Times*), 67, 69, 106
"The Great Baby," 64-65
Great Expectations, 16, 32, 35, 41, 56, 80, 104-7, 132-33; children in, as autobiographical, 108-29; economics in, 109-17, 120-25; educational values in, 112-13, 115-16, 120; father figure in, 119, 122; human values in human relatedness in, 126-27; self-awareness in, 110-13, 123-24
Greed, 58-76
Greene, Graham, 30
Gride, Arthur (*Nicholas Nickleby*), 42, 44, 63

Hard Times, 3, 11, 16, 49-50, 101, 104, 106
Hardy, Barbara, 97
Harmon, John (*Our Mutual Friend*), 45, 134
Havisham, Miss (*Great Expectations*), 105, 108, 115-16, 125
Headstone, Bradley (*Our Mutual Friend*), 131-33
Heathcliff (*Wuthering Heights*), 113-14
Heep, Uriah (*David Copperfield*), 80-83, 85, 92, 95-103, 109, 135
Hegel, Georg Wilhelm Friedrich, 10
Hexam, Charley (*Our Mutual Friend*), 10, 16, 45, 94, 131-33, 135-36
Hexam, Gaffer (*Our Mutual Friend*), 104

Hexam, Lizzie (*Our Mutual Friend*), 45, 52, 91, 105, 109, 131–36
Historicity, reality of, 6–10, 17
Hogarth, Mary, 54
House, Humphry, 149n13
Household Words, 25, 64–65, 69
Human values in human relatedness, 108–29

Ideology, 4–10, 12, 17, 24–25, 28–29, 62–101
India: development in, 17–18; social thinking in, 19–20
Industrialization, effects of, 46–57

Jackson, T. A., 10–12, 145n34
Jaggers (*Great Expectations*), 108, 112–13, 115–18; as father image, 119, 121–22, 125–26, 128
Jamaican insurrection, 145n40
James, Henry, 3, 141n2, 144n29
Jameson, Frederic, 6–7
Jarley, Mrs. (*The Old Curiosity Shop*), 47–48, 53
Jarndyce, John (*Bleak House*), 103
Johnson, Edgar, 149n10
Jonas (*Martin Chuzzlewit*), 58–59
Jones, Tom, 82, 94
Juvenile delinquency, 21–35

Kant, Immanuel, 5
Keats, John, 8
Kermode, Frank, 7, 146n53
Kettle, Arnold, 21–22, 24, 30, 114, 147nn1,3, 163n10
Kincaid, James R., 24–25, 81, 93
King Lear, 52, 70
Kingsley, Charles, 149n13
Kipling, Rudyard, 68
Kotzin, Michael C., 148n6
Krieger, Murray, 142n5
Kristeva, Julia, 6, 143n13, 146n54
Krook (*Bleak House*), 105

Lankford, William T., 147nn2–3
Laurie, Peter, 64

Lawrence, D. H., 48
Layard, Austen Henry, 64
Leavis, F. R., 3, 141n3, 156n17
"Leda and the Swan," 103
LeGuin, Ursula, 161n10
Letters, 64
Lévi-Strauss, Claude, 4
Linkinwater, Tim (*Nicholas Nickleby*), 43, 45
Linton, Edgar (*Wuthering Heights*), 113–15
Littimer (*David Copperfield*), 85, 89
Little Dorrit, 16, 101, 103–4, 106, 110
Little Nell Trent. *See* Trent, Nell
Lorry, Jarvis (*A Tale of Two Cities*), 104
Lucas, John, 79, 81, 97
Luddites and industrial revolution, 49
Lukács, Georg, 136–37

Macaulay, Thomas Babington, 50
Macherey, P., 142n6
McMaster, Juliet, 148n7
Magwitch, Abel (*Great Expectations*), 43, 51, 109, 111, 118; as father image, 122–26, 128
Maldon, Jack (*David Copperfield*), 82–83
Manheim, Leonard F., 90, 97, 158n24
Mann, Mrs. (*Oliver Twist*), 25, 34
Manning, Sylvia, 146n50
Marcus, Steven, 34, 39–40, 46, 51, 53, 148n7, 149nn16–17, 151n28, 152n9, 153n20, 155nn12–13
Marriage, capitalism and Victorian values, 66, 103, 105–6
Martin Chuzzlewit, 16, 39, 62–63; fortune hunters in, 58–60
Martyrdom, 36–57, 62, 71, 75
Marx, Karl, 130, 136
Maylie, Rose (*Oliver Twist*), 37
Mealy Potatoes (*David Copperfield*), 14, 107, 121
Measure for Measure, 134

Meckier, Jerome, 152nn12, 17
Meisel, Martin, 127
Melada, Ivan, 152n10
Mell, Mr. (David Copperfield), 84, 86–89
Merdle, Mr. and Mrs. (Little Dorrit), 103, 106
Metropolitan Sanitary Association, 26, 65
Micawber, Wilkins (David Copperfield), 91–96, 98–101, 108–9
Micawber, Mrs. Wilkins (David Copperfield), 78, 92–95
Middlemarch, 132
Milhauser, Milton, 127–29
Military commission purchased and military-industrial complexes, 65–66
Mill, John Stuart, 12
Miller, J. Hillis, 21, 53, 125, 147n2, 151n29
Monflathers, Miss (The Old Curiosity Shop), 49–50
Monks (Oliver Twist), 34, 56
Monod, Silvère, 151n7
Moral allegories, 62–101
Morfin (Dombey and Son), 104
Mother image, 78–79, 87–88, 92–95, 98, 100
Moynahan, Julian, 56
Mrs. Warren's Profession, 28–29, 33
Murdstones, Edward (David Copperfield), 80

Nancy (Oliver Twist), 28–29, 33–34
Needham, Gwendolyn, 78, 81–83, 94, 101
Nell. See Little Nell Trent
Nelson, Harland S., 155n12
Nicholas Nickleby, 16, 30, 62, 79; death of children in, 36–39, 41; exploitation of children in, 36–37, 40–42, 44–45; self-image in, 36–46; surrogate relations in, 39–46, 62
Nickleby, Kate, 42, 45

Nickleby, Mrs., 45
Nickleby, Nicholas, 16, 39–44, 50, 52, 55–57, 60, 62, 73, 75, 102, 135
Nickleby, Ralph, 40–45, 51, 55–56, 63, 66, 102
Nickleby, Smike, 38–43, 45–46, 52–53, 56, 63, 79, 100
Nietzsche, Friedrich, 6, 142n8
Noggs, Newman (Nicholas Nickleby), 43
Nubbles, Kit (The Old Curiosity Shop), 16, 39, 46–47, 50, 52, 54–57, 60, 62, 73, 76, 135

The Old Curiosity Shop, 16, 27, 30, 62–63, 79; death of children in, 46–57; religion in, 49, 53; romantic excesses of, 49–51; surrogate relations in, 46–47, 50–52, 54, 59; Victorian society portrayed in, 46–57
Oliver Twist, 9–10, 13, 15–16, 47, 49, 56, 61–64, 76, 79; Christian ethics in, 21–35; contradictions in, 22–23, 27; criminality in, 24–25, 30, 33–35; educational values in, 25–26; ideology of, 24–25, 28–29; plot and pattern of, 21–27, 30–32; religion and awaiting grace in, 23, 25–26, 33; social being, vision and adjustment in, 22–23, 26–27, 31, 33, 35; split self-image in, 36–38, 42
On This Side Idolatry, 12
Orwell, George, 10–12, 16, 146n51
"That Other Public," 64
Our Mutual Friend, 9, 16, 105–6; class distinction in, 130–38; communism and Victorian values in, 130, 135–37; educational values in, 133, 135

Pancks (Little Dorrit), 104–5, 106
Pearson, Gabriel, 46, 51
Pecksniff (Martin Chuzzlewit), 58–59

Peggotty, Clara (*David Copperfield*), 78
Peggotty, Daniel (*David Copperfield*), 78, 80–82, 88, 100–101
Peggotty, Emily (*David Copperfield*), 77, 83, 88, 90, 99
Peggotty, Ham (*David Copperfield*), 88, 90
People's Charter, 11
Pip. *See* Pirrip, Philip
Pipchin, Mrs., 73, 104
Pirrip, Philip (*Great Expectations*), 15–16, 43, 45, 51, 76, 88, 92, 105, 107–30, 132–33, 135–36
Pocket, Herbert (*Great Expectations*), 16, 108
Podsnap (Podsnappery) (*Our Mutual Friend*), 67, 130–33, 135–36, 138
"Preludes," 47, 77
"Prufrock," 47
Pumblechook (*Great Expectations*), 111

Quilp, Daniel (*The Old Curiosity Shop*), 46, 50, 52, 54–55, 66
"Quilpiad," 46

Racism, Eyre controversy, 12, 145n40
Radicalism, 11
Railroads and business practices, 65, 69–70, 75
Reform, social changes, 11–13, 21–35
Religion, 23, 25–26, 33, 49, 53
Richardson, Samuel, 53
Ricks, Christopher, 109, 121
Rigaud (*Little Dorrit*), 103
Robert, Bechofer, 12
Rokesmith, John (*Our Mutual Friend*), 130–31
Romantic associations, 49–51, 77, 80–83, 87–88, 90–91, 93, 98–101
Rugg (*Little Dorrit*), 105

Salem House, 84, 86–87, 91
Samson Agonistes, 4

Sartor Resartus, 77
Satis House, 112–13, 115–16, 120
Scholes, Robert, 4, 142n7
Self-awareness and image, 9, 16–17, 34–57, 62–101, 108–38
Shakespeare, William, 8, 134
Shaw, George Bernard, 28–29, 103
Sikes, Bill (*Oliver Twist*), 25, 27, 33, 38
Skewton, Mrs. (*Dombey and Son*), 74
Slum clearance, 21–35
Smike. *See* Nickleby, Smike
Smiles, Samuel, 103
Snobbishness, 81
Social being and artist, 21–35
Social breeding and moral survival, 77–101
Social mores, 46–57
Social perceptions, 62–76
Social reality in human relatedness, 127
Social reform, 11–13
Social vision and adjustment, 22–23, 26–27, 29, 31, 33, 35
Socialistic ideology, 12
Sophy. *See* Crewler, Sophy
Sowerberry (*Oliver Twist*), 32, 34, 36
Spenlow, Dora. *See* Copperfield, Dora (Spenlow)
Spenlow, Mr. (*David Copperfield*), 80, 108
Spilka, Mark, 80, 154n31
Squeers, Wackford (*Nicholas Nickleby*), 40, 42, 74, 104
Steerforth, James (*David Copperfield*), 16, 81–91, 96–97, 99–101, 108, 122
Stone, Harry, 148n6, 154n4
Strong, Annie (*David Copperfield*), 82–83
Strong, Doctor (*David Copperfield*), 82–83, 85, 88, 92
Studies in European Liberalism, 136
Summerson, Esther (*Bleak House*), 16, 76, 105–7, 109, 135

Surrogate relations, 39–47, 50–52, 57, 62–63, 81–91, 96–97, 99–101

Swiveller, Dick (*The Old Curiosity Shop*), 39, 46, 55, 57

Taine, Hippolyte, 75

A Tale of Two Cities, 11, 16, 104–6

Talon, Henri, 64, 154n4

Thackeray, William Makepeace, 53

Tigg, Montague (*Martin Chuzzlewit*), 59

Tillotson, Kathleen, 62, 148n6

"To Autumn," 109

Tom-All-Alone (*Bleak House*), 102

Toodle, Mr. (*Dombey and Son*), 49

Toodle, Polly (*Dombey and Son*), 15, 66–71, 131

Trabb, Mr. (*Great Expectations*), 110

Traddles, Tommy (*David Copperfield*), 16, 80–82, 91, 93–96, 100–101, 108

Trent, Little Nell's grandfather (*The Old Curiosity Shop*), 50–52, 55, 57, 63

Trent, Nell (*The Old Curiosity Shop*), 16, 38–39, 63, 73, 75, 79, 100, 134–35; and children and death, 46–57

Tristram Shandy, 8

Trotwood, Betsy (*David Copperfield*), 78–79, 87–88, 98, 100, 108

Twist, Oliver, 16, 60–61, 79–80, 100, 106–7, 111, 125–26, 133, 135–36; awaiting grace, 23, 25–26, 33; compared with Charles Hexam, 10, 108, 135–36; self-image of, 36–38, 41, 43, 50, 52–53, 56

Vanity Fair, 8

Veneering (*Our Mutual Friend*), 130–31, 133, 138

Victorian values: of capitalism and marriage, 63, 65, 68, 103, 105–6; of education and literature, 104; and fortune hunters, 58–60, 62–76; and Martin Chuzzlewit, 58–61; Marxist critique of, 130, 135–36; dramatized, 46–57

"The Waste Land," 104

"We Are Seven," 53

Wegg, Silas (*Our Mutual Friend*), 133

Wemmick (*Great Expectations*), 104, 119

Westlock, John (*Martin Chuzzlewit*), 58

Wickfield, Agnes (*David Copperfield*), 52, 57, 80, 82, 87–88, 90–91, 98–99, 108, 117, 128, 135

Wickfield, Mr. (*David Copperfield*), 95, 98–99, 108

Wilde, Oscar, 39

Wilfer, Bella (*Our Mutual Friend*), 45, 130, 133–35

Williams, Raymond, 11–12, 69, 145n38

Wilson, Angus, 37, 151n3

Wilson, Edmund, 3

Winters, Warrington, 153n29

Women, influence of, 77–83, 87–88, 90, 92, 98–101

Woodcourt, Allan (*Bleak House*), 105

Wordsworth, William, 53, 77

Wrayburn, Eugene (*Our Mutual Friend*), 45, 91, 105, 133

Wren, Jenny (*Our Mutual Friend*), 52, 108, 132–33

Writers and Leviathan, 12

Yeats, William Butler, 103

Zola, Emile, 138

COMPOSED BY METRICOMP, GRUNDY CENTER, IOWA
MANUFACTURED BY EDWARDS BROTHERS, INC.,
ANN ARBOR, MICHIGAN
TEXT AND DISPLAY LINES ARE SET IN PALATINO

Library of Congress Cataloging-in-Publication Data
Raina, Badri N., 1941–
Dickens and the dialectic of growth.
Bibliographical references: pp. 141–163.
Includes index.
1. Dickens, Charles, 1812–1870 — Political and social
views. 2. Social problems in literature. 3. Middle
class in literature. 4. Self in literature.
5. Deconstruction. 6. Marxist criticism. I. Title.
PR4592.S58R35 1986   823'.8   85-40767
ISBN 0-299-10610-1